Uncle Russ Chittenden's

# Good Ole Boys Wild Game Cookbook

or

*How To Cook
'Possum and Other Varmints Good*

Published by
Image Graphics, Inc.
Paducah, Kentucky
1989

Additional copies of this book may be ordered from:

Collector Books
5801 Kentucky Dam Rd.
Paducah, KY 42001

or

Good Ole Boys Cookbook
P.O. Box 8367
Paducah, KY 42002-8367

@ $14.95. Add 2.00 for postage and handling.
Copyright: Russ Chittenden, 1989

# Table Of Contents

# FOREWARD

Before the white man came, the Indians and Eskimos of North America were of necessity a provident people. Though not conservative of wildlife by design, they generally ate everything edible of their quarry and used the rest in various ways. The kill was the occasion for a tabagie or feast among the Iroquois. Often a camp was set up at the site of a major kill. Here the Indians gathered and feasted as long as the meat lasted.* Similar festivities were carried out by other primitive peoples across the continent . . . north to south . . . east to west.

And . . ., in modern day America, hunters and fishermen are still notoriously fond of getting together periodically in order to lie to one another, drink a lot and eat fattening foods. Thus was born "The Lair of the Ancient Hunter", a place where "Good Ole Boys" could gather to cook and eat the wild stuff gathering freezer burn at home . . . Good Ole Boys duped into marrying women with good legs . . . but whom they belatedly discovered could not or would not skin a coon or pick a goose . . . or cook anything not factory wrapped in plastic only a Russian weight lifter** could open.

Over a period of years, these Good Ole Boys have experimented with cooking and eating about everything they could semi-legally capture whether it slithered, swam, flew, walked or crawled.

The recipes contained herein were either developed here or borrowed from others who dropped in and . . . under the influence of alcohol divulged their secrets.

It would be next to impossible to publish the countless "favorite recipes" offered to us. A recipe for venison can usually be used for elk and moose and anything else that wears horns. A pheasant recipe, in turn, will work well on grouse, prairie chickens and the like.

One thing you can bank on . . . the finished product of these recipes will be good!

Uncle Russ Chittenden

---

\*     All skinning, cooking and camp clean-up was done by squaws
\*\*    or a 110 pound woman

*Well stocked refrigerator in the Lair of the Ancient Hunter. Good Ole Boys live "full" lives.*

*Product of local cabin industry. Good Ole Boys doing all American best to make the industry prosper . . .*

# Appropriate Wines, Beers and Ales

Since a game dinner for most people is not an every-day occasion, the bird or beast upon the table deserves its bottle... as does the cook or host or hostess who serves it.

In general, a dry red wine of good vintage is best accompaniment for venison, moose, antelope, caribou, elk and the like. A well aged Bordeau--Medoc, Pomerol, St. Emilion or a vintage California Cabernet will do nicely. You can substitute a Cotes du Rhone-Hermitage, Chateauneuf-du-Pape or one of the robust Burgundies from Cote de Beaune, Cote de Nuits, etc.

The red wines are also quite acceptable when served with wild boar and collared peccary or javelina.

Dark beers go well with rabbit especially hasenpfeffer and are good with venison roasts and stews.

The foregoing reds do well with ducks and geese and if you really want to show off, salute your goose or turkey with a robust Burgundy.

Pheasant and quail rate a Champaign or a white Burgundy. A white Burgundy also complements dove, snipe and the other white breasted birds.

Unfortunately, most of these delights aren't available in a six pack and will forever remain unknown to the Good Ole Boys of our aquaintance.

# Large
# Game

# Simple Pot Roast Of Venison

| | | | | |
|---|---|---|---|---|
| 1 | 3 lb. roast | | 1 | Cup hot water |
| 1 | envelope dry onion soup mix | | | Worchestershire sauce |

Place the roast in a pot or glass casserole dish.

In another bowl mix the dry soup mix with enough water to make a paste. Brush it over the roast. Now, sprinkle the roast liberally with the Worchestershire sauce. Pour the cup of hot water into the bottom of the pot, cover and cook in a 275 degree oven for two (2) hours or until tender. Transfer to a hot platter, slice and pour the sauce over same.

Serves 4.

# Venison Pot Roast

| | | | | |
|---|---|---|---|---|
| 4-5 | lb. deer rump roast | | 1 | bay leaf |
| 1/4 | Cup flour | | 1 | Tbs red wine vinegar |
| 1/4 | tsp salt | | 4 | potatoes, quartered |
| 1/2 | tsp black pepper | | 4 | carrots, cut into 1" chunks |
| 1/2 | lb. salt pork, diced | | 10 | small white onions |
| 2 1/2 | Cups water | | | |

Mix the flour, salt and pepper and rub it into the meat.

Render a half cup of fat from the diced salt pork in a dutch oven. Brown the meat on all sides in the fat. Add the water, vinegar and bay leaf. Cover, and cook slowly until tender, probably 3 hours, in a 250 degree oven. Add potatoes and carrots for last 30 minutes. Toss in a quartered turnip if one is available.

Serves 8-10.

# Roast Venison With Mushrooms

| | |
|---|---|
| 4-5 | lb. rump roast |
| 1 | 10 3/4 oz. can cream of mushroom soup |
| 1 | 4 oz. can mushroom bits and pieces |
| 4 | medium size potatoes, scrubbed, not peeled |
| | salt & pepper |

Place the roast on a large piece of aluminum foil and put it in a roasting pan. Pour the soup over the roast and sprinkle with a little salt and pepper. Close the foil around the roast and place in an oven preheated to 350 degrees. Roast for 1 1/2 hours and remove from oven. Open the foil and add the potatoes (which have been halved) and the mushrooms. Re-seal the foil and roast for another hour. Thin slice the roast, pour the mushroom sauce over it and serve.

Serves 6.

## Venison Roast And Mushrooms

| | |
|---|---|
| 2-3 | lb. neck or shoulder roast |
| 1 | 8 oz. can mushrooms, drained |
| 1 | 10 3/4 oz. can condensed cream of mushroom soup |
| 1 | medium onion, sliced |
| 1/2 | tsp salt |
| 1/4 | tsp pepper |
| | cooking oil |

Brown the roast on all sides in a little cooking oil. Transfer the roast to a covered pot and sprinkle with the salt and pepper. Add the condensed soup and the mushrooms. Lay the onions on top. Cover and cook in a 325 degree oven for 1 1/2 hours. Transfer the roast to a hot platter, slice and pour the pan juices over same.

Serves 4.

## Hot & Spicy Venison Pot Roast

| | | | | |
|---|---|---|---|---|
| 3-4 | lb. roast | 1 | 8 oz. can tomato sauce |
| 2 | medium onions, chopped | 1/4 | tsp nutmeg |
| 1 | tsp garlic powder | 1/2 | tsp poultry seasoning |
| 6 | Tbs butter or margarine | 1/4 | tsp cinnamon |
| 1/3 | Cup vinegar | 1/4 | tsp allspice |

Saute' the onions and garlic powder in the butter in a skillet until the onions are transparent. Remove them and keep hot while searing the roast on all sides until brown in the same skillet. Transfer the roast to a heavy lidded pot, cover with the onions and add the vinegar and tomato sauce. Sprinkle the seasonings over the meat and cook covered for 2 hours in a 300 degree oven. Slice on a hot platter and pour the pan juices over same.

Serves 4-6.

# Aluminum Foiled Venison Pot Roast

| | | | | |
|---|---|---|---|---|
| 2-3 | lb. roast | 1/2 | tsp black pepper |
| 1 1/4 | Cup water | 1/2 | tsp salt |
| 1 | envelope dry onion soup mix | 1/4 | tsp cayenne pepper |

Place the roast in the center of a square sheet of heavy duty aluminum foil. Bring the edges up to form a pouch or envelope. Pour the water over the roast. Add the soup mix, salt and pepper evenly over top of the roast. Pinch together the edges of the aluminum foil to form a tight seal. Place the pouch in a shallow baking pan and roast for 1 1/2 hours in a 325 degree oven. Remove roast to a hot platter and slice it thin. Ladle the gravy over the meat or potatoes or noodles you may serve as accompaniment.

Serves 4.

# Grassy Lake Venison Pot Roast

| | |
|---|---|
| 3-5 | lbs. rump or shoulder of venison |
| 4 | Tbs flour |
| 4 | Tbs brown sugar |
| 1 | tsp paprika |
| 1/2 | tsp black pepper |
| 6 | Tbs sweet butter |
| 1/2 | Cup venison or beef stock, (hot melt a bouillon cube) |
| 2 | ribs celery, chopped |
| 1 | onion, chopped |
| 1 | onion per person, quartered (optional) |
| 1 | potato per person, quartered (optional) |

Blend flour, brown sugar, paprika, and pepper; sprinkle over the meat. Brown meat in butter in a Dutch oven. Add stock, celery, and onion. Cover, roast at 375 degrees for 3 1/2 to 4 hours. Quartered onions and potatoes can be added for last half hour, if desired.

Serves 6 to 8 half drunk outdoor types or 10 to 12 persons of more gentle breeding.

*This is a mainstay on the menu in the Lair of the Ancient Hunter. We generally accompany it with Yellow Squash Casserole (page 98), Duck Camp Celery (page 101), and Spiced Carrots (page 99).*

# Cranberried Roast Of Deer

| | | | | |
|---|---|---|---|---|
| 3-4 | lbs. deer roast | 2 | Cups cranberries |
| 1/4 | lb. salt pork | 2 | Tbs sugar |
| 1 | tsp black pepper | 1 | onion, stuck with 2-3 cloves |
| 1/2 | Cup flour | | |

Remove most of the fat from the meat. Mix the flour and pepper and dredge the meat in the mixture. Rub it in well.

Dice the salt pork and fry it in a Dutch oven over medium heat. When it turns a crisp gold, remove the pork with a slotted spoon. Brown the roast on all sides in the hot fat.

While the meat is browning, boil the cranberries in a cup of water until the skin pops. Pour the cranberries and juice over the meat. Scatter the diced salt pork over the top and sprinkle 1 Tbs sugar over that. Add the onion. Cover and simmer for 2 1/2-3 hours, or until the meat is tender. The liquid around the roast should be simmering, never boiling. Add a little water if necessary to prevent it cooking dry. Transfer the meat to a warm platter and keep it hot.

Remove the onion and strain the sauce, add the remaining sugar, bring to a low boil and thicken with a mixture of 1/2 cup warm water and 2 tsp flour. Serve the sauce with the roast.

Serves 8.

## Saddle Of Venison

*Saddles from older deer should be marinated before roasting. See Bubba's Red Game Marinade on page 90. Marinating is not needed if venison is from a young animal.*

| | | | |
|---|---|---|---|
| 1 | saddle of venison | 6 | Tbs softened butter or margarine, melted |
| 1/2 | tsp black pepper | | red wine |
| 1/2 | tsp Tabasco | 2 | Cups beef bouillon |
| 1 | tsp thyme | | Beurre Manie' |
| 1 1/2 | tsp salt | 1/2 | Cup Madeira |

Rub the saddle well with the pepper, Tabasco, thyme, salt and softened butter. Place in a shallow pan and roast at 450 degrees for 30 minutes. Reduce heat to 400 degrees and continue roasting until 125 degrees is registered on a meat thermometer (125 degrees for rare; 140 degrees for medium), about 10-12 minutes per pound. Baste several times with a 50-50 mix of melted butter and red wine. Transfer the saddle to a hot platter and let it stand in a warm place for about 15 minutes before carving.

In a saucepan, bring the bouillon to a boil, stir in the Buerre Manie' and any pan juices left during the roasting process. Continue stirring until thickened. Add the Madeira and let the sauce simmer 5-8 minutes. Correct the seasoning.

Serves 6. Serve with candied sweet potatoes and Spicy Red Cabbage (page 100)

# Venison Chops In Foil

8     venison chops about 1/2" thick
8     slices cold boiled ham 1/4"-3/8" thick
1     stick butter or margarine
2     medium onions, chopped fine
12    medium mushrooms, sliced
2     Tbs minced fresh parsley
1/2  tsp salt
1/2  tsp pepper
8     Tbs sour cream
      heavy aluminum foil

Melt 1/2 the butter in a large heavy skillet and saute the chops for about 10 minutes. Remove to a heated platter and keep warm. Melt remaining butter in skillet and saute onions, mushrooms and parsley until golden. Sprinkle with salt and pepper.

Prepare foil packets. Cut 8 pieces of foil about 12" x 14" each. On each piece, place 1 piece of ham topped with a venison chop. Top these with 2 heaping Tbs of the onion- mushroom-parsley mixture. Add a Tbs of the sour cream and seal. Bake in a preheated 350 degree oven for 20 minutes. Serve in the foil. Serve with Baked Stuffed Mushrooms (page 97) and Po' Folks Spiced Cabbage (page 100).


# Clarence Ray's Stovetop Round Steak

2     pounds round steak           1/4  tsp salt
      commercial meat tenderizer    3     Tbs cooking oil
3     Tbs flour                   1 1/2 Cups water
1/4  tsp black pepper

Tenderize the steak by piercing it deeply with a fork, then sprinkle each side with a commercial meat tenderizer. Allow it to stand for about an hour before you pound it to uniform thickness with a meat hammer.

Mix the flour, salt and pepper together. Then gently pound the mixture into both sides of the steak with the smooth side of the meat hammer.

Brown both sides of the steak in the cooking oil over medium heat. Them add the water, cover, reduce the heat to low and simmer for 1 hour. Transfer to a hot platter. Serve with French Fried Onion Rings (page 96).

Serves 4.

# Stove Top Venison In Onion Gravy

2  venison steaks, about 1/2" thick
   flour
   salt & pepper to taste
1  Cup vegetable oil
1  medium onion, chopped
2  tsp instant beef bouillon
1  tsp Worcestershire sauce
   water

Dredge the steaks in flour seasoned with salt and pepper (cover well). Brown the steaks on both sides in oil in a skillet. Remove steaks and set aside.

Pour off most of the oil, leaving about 2 tablespoons in the skillet. Saute chopped onion in the oil until tender. Blend in 1 Tbs flour and brown same while stirring constantly. Add the bouillon, Worcestershire sauce and enough water to make a thin gravy. Cook this mess until well blended and slightly thickened, stirring all the time. Return steaks to the skillet, put a lid on it and simmer for an hour and forty minutes.

Serves 4.

# Venison Swiss Steak From The Yancy Place

1  venison steak, (2 lbs. or thereabouts), 1" thick
3  Tbs flour
1  stick butter or margarine
1  medium onion (yellow), coarsely chopped
1  small green pepper, seeded and coarsely chopped
1  stalk celery, sliced in 1/4" rounds
1  16 oz. can peeled tomatoes
2  Cups beef Consomme' or beef bouillon
1  tsp salt
2  crushed peppercorns

With a meat mallet, saucer or similar weapon, pound the flour into the meat on both sides. Over high heat melt butter in a large skillet and quickly brown steak on both sides. Put all the vegetables in a tightly lidded pot or Dutch oven and place steaks on top of them. Pour in the skillet drippings and the consomme'. Add salt and peppercorns. Cover and simmer until meat is tender . . . about 1 1/2 hours. Serve with fluffy whipped potatoes, and buttered broad noodles or over white rice.

Serves 4.

*The Yancy Place Hunting Club provides fantastic Canada goose hunting adjacent to the Ballard Wildlife Management Area in far Western Kentucky. Guests here are subjected to some of the finest eating in North America. Entrees such as this are served regularly at gatherings of rednecks, good ole boys, duck and goose hunters and similar ne'er-do-wells held here.*

# Venison And Rice

2     lbs. venison round steak, all fat removed
1/2   Cup soy sauce
2     cloves garlic (or 2 Tbs garlic juice)
1     Tbs fresh ginger or 1 tsp ground
1/2   Cup salad oil
2     Cups green onion, thinly sliced
2     Cups red or green peppers cut into 1" squares
4     stalks celery, thinly sliced
2     Tbs cornstarch
2     Cups water
4     tomatos, cut into wedges

Cut the venison across grain into strips 1/8" thick. Combine soy sauce, garlic and ginger. Add the venison, toss and set aside.

Heat the oil in a large skillet over high heat. Add the venison and toss until browned. Cover and simmer for 30-40 minutes over low heat. Turn heat up and add vegetables. Toss until vegetables are tender crisp, 10-15 minutes. Mix cornstarch with water. Add to skillet; stir and cook until thickened. Add the tomato wedges and heat through. Serve with (over) white rice.

Serves 8.

# Bayou Venison And Rice

1     lb ground venison
1     onion, chopped
1     green pepper, chopped
1/4   Cup vegetable oil
1     16 oz. can tomatos
1     16 oz. can red kidney beans

1     Tbs black pepper
2     Tbs chili powder
1/4   tsp garlic salt
1     tsp salt
1     Tbs mustard
3     Cups white rice, cooked

Brown the venison, onion and green pepper in the vegetable oil in a Dutch oven (deep iron skillet) or something. Add other ingredients except rice and bring to a boil, covered, over high heat . . . turn down heat and simmer for 30 minutes; stir frequently. Serve over hot rice to about 8 'possum hunters or reasonably accurate facsimiles.

# Barlow Bottoms Venison Stew

| | |
|---|---|
| 2 | lbs. deer meat trimmed and cut into 1" cubes |
| 3 | Tbs butter or margarine |
| 2 | Tbs olive oil |
| 1 | lb small onions, peeled and whole |
| 2 | Tbs claret wine |
| 2 | Tbs white vinegar |
| 4 | Tbs tomato paste |
| 2 | tsp salt |
| 1/2 | tsp black pepper |
| 2 | Cups hot water |
| 4 | garlic cloves, unpeeled |
| 2 | Tbs pickling spices, tied in cheesecloth |

Heat the butter and oil in a skillet, add the meat and brown it on all sides. Remove the meat to a heavy Dutch oven. Add the onions to the skillet and brown in the hot oil. Add to the meat in the Dutch oven.

Combine the remaining ingredients (except the pickling spice) in a bowl. Stir well and pour the mixture over the meat. Place the pickling spice bag in the center of the stew. Bring to a boil. Cover and reduce heat. Simmer for 2-2 1/2 hours, or until the meat is tender. Remove the spice bag after about an hour. Thicken the stew with a thin water-flour paste about 5 minutes before serving.

Serves 6.


# Deer Camp Stew

| | | | |
|---|---|---|---|
| 1 1/2 | lb cubed venison | 1/4 | tsp thyme |
| | shortening | 1/4 | tsp sweet basil |
| 1/4 | tsp garlic juice | 1/2 | Cup tomato catsup |
| 2 | medium red onions, chopped | 3 | carrots, chopped |
| 1 | can tomato soup | 3 | stalks celery, chopped |
| 1 | Cup Burgundy | 4-6 | medium potatoes, cubed |

Brown venison in about 3 Tbs of shortening in a large skillet. Lower heat. Add onions, garlic juice, salt and pepper. Saute until onions are transparent. Add soup, Burgundy, basil, thyme, catsup; stir well. Simmer, covered for 10 minutes. Add vegetables and simmer for 2 hours more.

# Crockpot Venison Stew

| 2 | pounds stew venison | 1/2 | tsp paprika |
| 6 | carrots, scraped & chunked | 1/4 | tsp black pepper |
| 4 | potatoes, peeled & chunked | 1 | tsp salt |
| 4 | zucchini, chunked | 1 | Cup beef bouillon |
| 2 | medium onions, chunked | 1/4 | Cup flour |
| 1 | tsp Worchestershire sauce | 1/4 | Cup water |

Put all items except flour and water in the crockpot, cover and cook at least 5 hours on low setting.

Mix water and flour, pour into stew and turn to high setting for 15 minutes or until slightly thickened. Serve with Yellow Squash Casserole (page 98) and Po Folks Spiced Cabbage (page 100).

Serves 6.

# Venison Fried Hash

| 2 | Cups tender cooked venison, chopped fine |
| 4 | Cups mashed potatoes |
| 1 | tsp salt |
| 1 | saltspoon pepper |

Mix 'til there are no lumps. Put six (6) Tbs of hot water in a spider; melt in two (2) Tbs butter. Put in hash. Let it simmer slowly until it has absorbed the water and formed a brown crust. Do not stir. Fold over as you would an omelet and turn on a hot platter.

*You'll probably wind up with two burned fingers and half of the hash on the stove or floor . . . Your guests will think it's worth the sacrifice.*

# Leftover Venison Pie

| | |
|---|---|
| 2 | Cups cooked venison, cut in 1/2" to 1" pieces |
| 1/2 | Cup cooked (boiled) onions |
| 1 | Cup cooked carrots, cut in 1" long chunks |
| 1 | Cup boiled potatoes, cut in 1 1/2" chunks |
| 1 | Cup beef gravy (Pillsbury Brown Gravy Mix does well) |
| 1/4 | Cup butter |
| 2 | tsp baking powder |
| 1 | tsp salt |
| 1 1/2 | Cups milk |
| 1 | 4 oz. pkg. grated cheddar cheese |
| 1 | Tbs dried minced onions |
| 1 | Tbs sugar |

Combine the first five ingredients and set aside.

Melt the butter in an 8" square baking dish in the oven. Combine remaining ingredients in mixing bowl, stir until blended well and pour into the baking dish. Pour the venison mixture over the batter without stirring. Bake at 350 degrees for 1 hour.

Serves 6.

# Creamed Deerburgers With Potatoes

| | |
|---|---|
| 1 | lb deerburger |
| 2 | Tbs milk |
| 2 | tsp flour |
| 1 | 10 3/4 oz. can condensed cream of mushroom soup |
| 1 | 4 oz. can mushrooms, drained |
| 1 | 14 1/2 oz. can beef broth |
| 5 | medium potatoes, cut into 1" chunks |
| 1/2 | tsp salt |
| 1/2 | tsp black pepper |
| | cooking oil |

Shape deerburgers the usual size. Dip each in milk; then in the flour. Brown deerburgers in a skillet with a little cooking oil. Add the remaining items. Cover and cook over low heat until the potatoes are done . . . about 30 minutes.

Serves 4.

# Deerburger And Rice

1     lb ground venison
3     Tbs vegetable oil
1     5 oz. can button mushrooms
2     Cups water
1     5 oz. pkg. Uncle Ben's Long Grain & Wild Rice w/ Beef Stock Sauce with
         Vegetables
1/3  Cup bell pepper, chopped fine
1/4  tsp salt
3     Tbs sour cream (optional)

Heat oil in a skillet over high heat. Add the meat and cook, stirring, until no longer pink. Add the mushrooms, bell pepper and water. Stir in the contents of rice and seasoning packages and salt. Bring to a boil. Reduce heat, cover and simmer 5-7 minutes or until most of the liquid is absorbed. She's ready to eat. However, if you really want something great remove from heat and stir in the sour cream. Serve with Duck Camp Celery (page 101) and Spiced Carrots (page 99).

Will serve 4 or 5.


# Venison Chili

6    Tbs butter or margarine
6    medium onions, sliced
3    lbs. ground venison
2    28 oz. cans tomatoes
1    6 oz. can tomato paste
1    Cup beer
1    Tbs salt
1/2  tsp Tabasco
3    Tbs chili powder
1/2  lb. spaghetti (optional)

Melt the butter or margarine in a large saucepan. Add the onions and cook at medium heat until transparent not brown. Add the ground venison and cook until lightly brown . . . break it up with a fork. Add the tomatoes, tomato paste, beer, salt, Tabasco and chili powder. Lower heat and simmer for 45-50 minutes.

If spaghetti is used, prepare according to package directions and add during the last 15 minutes of cooking time.

Serves 8.

# Venison Meatloaf

| | | | | |
|---|---|---|---|---|
| 2 | pounds deerburger | 1/2 | tsp sage |
| 1 1/3 | Cups milk | 1/2 | tsp black pepper |
| 1 | Cup bread crumbs | 1/2 | tsp thyme |
| 2 | eggs, beaten | 1/2 | tsp rosemary |
| 1/3 | Cup chopped onion | 1 | 8 oz. can tomato sauce |
| 1 1/4 | tsp salt | | |

Soak the breadcrumbs in the milk. Add rest of the stuff except the tomato sauce and mix well with your hands. Form into a loaf and place in a bread pan. Pour the tomato sauce over the loaf. Bake at 325 degrees for about 1 hour and 15 minutes.

Serves 8.

*Clean your fingernails.*

# Spiced Venison Burgers

1  pound ground venison
1/2  pound mild pork sausage
1  slice stale white bread, cut in 1/2" cubes
1  egg, beaten
1  medium onion, minced
1  Tbs margarine
  salt & pepper (preferably freshly ground) to taste
1  Tbs dry sweet basil
  red wine
  vegetable oil

Combine the venison and sausage.

Soak the cubed bread in the beaten egg. Saute the onion in the margarine, let it cool and add it to the meat mixture. Add the bread-egg mixture, salt, pepper and basil and 2 Tbs of the wine. Mix well. Mould into patties about 1" thick; should get 8-10.

Heat the vegetable oil in a large iron skillet at medium heat and brown the patties on each side, turning once. Turn the heat down to low. Sprinkle 1/2 Cup of wine over the patties, cover and cook slowly until no pink shows in the center of a patty . . . 15-20 minutes perhaps. Transfer to a heated platter and serve with buns, mustard, mayonnaise or the relish of your choosing.

# Deer Burgers
## (For Toothless Old Men)

| | | | |
|---|---|---|---|
| 1 | pound ground venison | 1 1/2 | Tbs flour |
| 1 | medium onion, chopped | | salt & pepper to taste |
| 1 | green pepper, chopped | | cheese slices |
| 1 | can peeled tomatos | 1 1/2 | Tbs vegetable oil |

Shape the venison into patties and brown on both sides in a skillet (big deep one) with the onions, vegetable oil and green pepper. Reduce temperature and cook for 20 minutes with lid on. Add tomatos and bring to a boil Reduce heat.

Blend flour with a small amount of water in a bowl; stir into sauce. Season with salt and pepper. Cook until thick stirring constantly . . . maybe 10 minutes. Top each patty with a slice of American cheese a few minutes before serving. Serve when cheese is melted.

Serves 4.


# Ontario Sweet And Sour Moose

| | |
|---|---|
| 4 | lbs. moose, cut up for stewing |
| 4 | beef bouillon cubes, melted in 4 Cups of water |
| | (can substitute 4 Cups beef consomme' or beef stock) |
| 2 | tsp salt |
| 2 | Tbs sugar |
| 1 | tsp cinnamon |
| 1 | tsp powdered cloves |
| 1 | tsp allspice |
| 1/4 | tsp nutmeg |
| 2 | Tbs butter or margarine |
| 2 | Tbs flour |
| 1 | Cup wine vinegar |
| 1 | Cup finely chopped onion |

Put meat, stock, salt, cloves, sugar, cinnamon, allspice and nutmeg in a heavy Dutch oven. Bring to a boil, cover, lower heat and simmer until meat is tender, about 2 hours. Remove from heat. Drain and reserve stock.

During last 30 minutes of the cooking period, melt butter in a saucepan and blend in flour. Slowly add the vinegar, stirring over medium heat, blend till smooth. Add onion and simmer for 30 minutes.

Now add the stock from meat to the sauce and cook for 15 minutes longer. Add to meat, heat through.

Serves 8. Serve with Spaetzle (page 104).

# Pot Roast Of Wyoming Elk

| | | | |
|---|---|---|---|
| 4-5 | lbs. elk roast | 1 | medium onion, sliced |
| 1 | Cup navy beans | 3 | ribs of celery, diced |
| | vegetable oil | 3 | carrots, sliced in 1" chunks |
| | salt & pepper | 1/2 | tsp garlic powder |
| 1 | 12 oz. can of warm beer | | flour |

Trim away most of the fat and wipe with a damp cloth. Place the beans in a saucepan and cover with boiling water. Let stand for two hours. Drain.

Pour vegetable oil in a large Dutch oven to a depth of 1/8" and heat. Brown the roast on all sides. Pepper the meat lightly while browning. Pour off excess vegetable oil and add water to a depth of 1/2". Cover and simmer for 1/2 hour. Now pour half the beer over the meat . . . slowly.

Drain the beans and add them to the pot along with the sliced onion. If the beans are not "just covered" with liquid add some water. Cover and simmer for about 2 hours.

Slowly pour the remaining beer over the meat and add the celery and carrots. Salt and pepper to taste and toss in a 1/2 tsp of garlic powder. Recover and simmer for another hour or until the meat is tender and the beans cooked.

Transfer the roast to a heated platter and keep it warm. Thicken the remaining bean sauce by stirring a thin flour/water paste into it. Slice the roast and serve with the sauce over broad noodles or hot cooked rice.

# Idaho Roasted Big Horn Sheep

| | | | |
|---|---|---|---|
| 3-5 | lbs. top round roast | 1 1/2 | tsp brown sugar |
| 2 | tsp garlic juice | 1/2 | tsp salt |
| 2 | tsp onion juice | 1/2 | tsp pepper |
| 2 | Cups tomato juice, warmed | 2 | Tbs all purpose flour |
| 4 | Tbs sweet butter | | |
| 1 | 10 3/4 oz. can undiluted cream of mushroom soup | | |

Rub meat with garlic and onion juice. Place on a rack in a roasting pan and add 1 Cup of tomato juice with the butter melted in it. Roast at 325 degrees for approximately 3 hours, basting with the pan juices every 30 minutes. Dissolve the brown sugar in the remaining Cup of tomato juice and add to the pan. Increase heat to 400 degrees and baste every 5-10 minutes to brown. Season with salt and pepper before serving.

Prepare a sauce by blending flour with soup in a saucepan over low heat, then mixing with pan juices.

Serves 8.

# Old Baldy's
## Roasted Leg Of Montana Pronghorn

| | | | |
|---|---|---|---|
| 4-5 | lbs. leg roast, boned | 1 1/2 | tsp pepper |
| 1/2 | Cup olive oil | 1 | bay leaf |
| 2 | Cups red wine | 3 | garlic cloves, minced |
| 4 | Tbs lemon juice | 2 | garlic cloves, slivered |
| 2 | tsp salt | | |

Marinate the roast for 48 hours in a mixture of all items except the slivered garlic. Turn several times during the marinating. Remove meat and drain. Cut slits in the meat and insert the garlic slivers. Let stand for 2-3 hours. Roast in a 200 degree oven for about 8 hours basting with the marinade from time to time. Serve well chilled.

Serves 8-10.

*Since the pronghorn's diet may include big helpings of sagebrush, the meat may have a robust flavor and . . . since the flavor concentrates in the fat, it makes it extra important to trim off all possible fat before marinating.*


# Bears In General
*Fall bears are usually quite fat just before hibernation both outside and in. They can provide the hunter with some succulent eating. The meat will be a little too oily for most palates if this fat isn't reduced. The outside fat can be trimmed without much trouble. The intramuscular fat can be removed from the pan as the cooking proceeds.*


# Broiled Bear Steak

| | |
|---|---|
| 2 | lbs. bear steak, 1-1 1/2" thick |
| | Red Wine Marinade (page 91) |
| 1/4 | Cup vegetable oil |
| | salt |
| | black pepper, preferably fresh ground |
| | crushed dried sage |
| 4 | large onions, sliced thin |
| 1/2 | stick butter or margarine |

Remove all fat. Marinate for 24-72 hours in Red Wine Marinade, turning meat whenever you think of it. Drain; pat dry. Brush with vegetable oil on both sides and sprinkle liberally with salt, pepper and sage. Broil for 15 minutes on each side or until well done.

Meanwhile, saute' onions in butter until golden. Serve steak with onions on top.

Serves 4.

# Ontario Skillet Fried Bear Steak

| | | | |
|---|---|---|---|
| 1 | steak, cut 1-1 1/2" thick | 6 | Tbs cooking oil |
| 1/4 | Cup chili sauce | 1 | Cup onion, sliced |
| 1 | tsp sage | | salt & pepper to taste |
| 1 | tsp ginger | | |

Mix chili sauce, sage and ginger and spread thickly on both sides of meat several hours before frying. Let stand at room temperature.

Heat cooking oil until it bubbles. Add steak and fry 5 minutes per side. Reduce heat and remove steak. Saute' onions until golden in same skillet. Return meat, cover and cook over medium-low heat until tender. Adjust seasonings and serve on a warm platter.

Serves 4. Serve with anything you would use to accompany a pork steak.

# Pot Roast Of Black Bear

| | | | |
|---|---|---|---|
| 3-4 | lb bear roast | 1 | medium onion, sliced |
| | oil for browning | 2 | bay leaves |
| 4 | Cups red wine | 1/4 | tsp crushed black peppercorns |

Remove every bit of fat possible. Mix wine, onion, bay leaves and peppercorns to make a marinade. Place the roast in a deep glass or ceramic bowl and pour the marinade over. Turn every now and then, if you think of it. Refrigerate overnight.

Thirty minutes before cooking, remove the roast from the marinade and pat dry with paper towels.

Heat the oil in a large Dutch oven and brown meat on all sides. Cover and bake in a 250 degree oven for one hour per pound. Baste with the marinade every hour.

Serve with sauerkraut, Old Folks Skellion's Thunder and Lightening (page 104) and mashed potatoes.

Serves 12-14, if you tell guests its bear. Serves 6-8, if you tell them its pork.

# Water Smoker Buffalo, Venison, Elk and Moose Roasts

Charcoal pan full, water pan full.

If roast (5-9 lbs.) is from an animal you know or guess to be over 18 months old, marinate overnight in Bubba's Red Game Marinade (page 90).

Remove all second skin and fat from the roast. With a sharp knife make incisions for insertion of strips of bacon and garlic slivers. Make at least one incision for every pound of meat. Grease the outside of the roast with bacon grease. Sprinkle with garlic salt and black pepper. Lay strips of bacon, onion and lemon on top of the meat and secure with toothpicks. Pour 1/2 cup of non-sweet burgundy wine in the water pan and smoke-cook 6-7 hours. Replenish water (use hot water) at 4 hours into the cooking cycle. Pour through grill without removing roast. Get the lid back on quickly.

# Hunter's Game Stew

| | |
|---|---|
| 2 | lbs. buffalo roast (tenderfeet can substitute beef) |
| 2 | lbs. Collared Rio Grande Peccary (can substitute pork) |
| 2 | lbs. pheasant, cut up |
| 2 | mallard ducks, cut up |
| 12 | doves or Baptist church pigeons |
| 1 | rabbit, cut up |
| 3 | quarts canned sliced tomatos |
| 3 | quarts corn (cream style) |
| 1/4 | Cup Worcestershire sauce |
| 1 | Tbs Tabasco sauce |
| 4 | lbs potatoes, diced large |

Place buffalo, peccary, pheasants, ducks, doves, and rabbit in large sauce pan. Add two (2) gallons spring water. Cook until meats are very tender, adding enough water to maintain two gallons of stock. Drain and reserve stock. Remove all bones and fat from meat.

Combine tomatos, corn, Worcestershire sauce, Tabasco sauce, boned meat and reserved stock in large pot. Simmer for four (4) hours or longer. Add the potatoes the last hour. Will yield 5-6 gallons . . . feed a crowd.

# Pachyderm Fricassee

| | | | |
|---|---|---|---|
| 1 | large elephant | | salt and pepper |
| | Bubba's Red Game Marinade | 2 | rabbits |
| | Brown Gravy | | |

Cut elephant in bite size pieces and marinate overnight in Bubba's Red Game Marinade (page 90). Remove and pat dry with paper towels.

Place the meat in a large Dutch oven. Add brown gravy to cover and salt and pepper to taste. Cook over a wood fire for about 4 weeks at 465 degrees F.

If guests drop in unexpectedly, add the rabbits for the last hour. and adjust seasonings. Do this only if necessary as most folks do not like to find hare in their stew.

Serves 3,400.

* We generally used Franco American prepared brown gravy . . . buy it by the case in 10-1/4 oz. cans.

## Cousin Barbara's Stuffed Camel

| | |
|---|---|
| 1 | medium size camel (Dromedaries have sweeter meat) |
| 1 | 90# lamb |
| 20 | Frying size chickens (Rhode Island Reds are best) |
| 60 | ostrich eggs |
| 12 | kilos* rice |
| 2 | kilos pine nuts |
| 2 | kilos almonds |
| 1 | kilo pistachio nuts |
| 110 | gallons water |
| | salt to taste |
| 5 | Tbs black pepper (fresh ground) |

Skin, trim and clean the camel, lamb and chickens and boil in a large pot until tender. Cook rice until fluffed according to package directions. Hard boil and peel the eggs. Then . . . stuff the chickens with the eggs and some rice. Stuff the lamb with 5 of the chickens and some rice. Stuff the camel with the lamb and more rice. Broil in a large oven until brown.

Now spread the remaining rice on a large platter and place the camel on top. Place the remaining stuffed chickens around the camel. Garnish with remaining boiled eggs and nuts.

Serves 1,215. Serve with collard greens and baked sweet potatoes.

*Cousin Barbara Martin traveled Africa for several years and collected recipes for many native dishes. We included only those for game we thought might be more readily available to the average hunter.*

* kilo or kiloliter = 10 hectoliters or 216.42 gallons

# Mountain Goat

The trophy Mountain Goat is a mature lean animal and is usually tougher'n most of us good ole boys have teeth to handle. He's gotta be marinated in something like Bubba's Red Game Marinade (page 90) for 3-4 days–and this after hanging for 10-12 days in a dry place, just above freezing.

Cooking can then be done by any recipe normally used for venison, antelope or wild mountain sheep.

*Our good ole boys suggest you do all of the above . . . then invite your wife's relatives over for dinner . . . They may show up in great numbers. They won't the next time.*

# Stovetop Caribou Steak

| | | | |
|---|---|---|---|
| 1 | caribou steak 1/2"-3/4" thick | 3 | Tbs port wine |
| 3 | Tbs butter | 1 | Tbs red currant jelly |
| | cayenne pepper | | salt |

Cut steak into pieces about 2" square. Salt to taste and place in a skillet with the butter. Brown each side quickly over high heat. Then lower heat, dust the meat with cayenne, add the wine and jelly, cover and simmer until pink on the inside when cut with a knife.

# Small
# Game
# Animals

# Fried Rabbit

2     cottontail rabbits (2-3 lbs. each), cut into serving pieces
       juice from half a lemon
       salt & pepper
1/4    tsp dried oregano
4     Tbs milk
2     eggs, lightly beaten
1/2    Cup flour
1/2    Cup fine bread crumbs
       cooking oil

Put rabbit pieces in water to cover with the lemon juice and parboil for 10 minutes. Drain, pat dry and sprinkle with salt, pepper and oregano. Combine milk and egg. Dip rabbit in flour, then in egg and then in bread crumbs. Heat oil 1/2" deep in a large skillet till a cube of bread turns golden in 1 minute. Brown rabbit on all sides. Lower heat and cook (covered) till tender . . . probably 25-30 minutes. Add 3 Tbs water for last 10 minutes. Drain and serve.

Serves 6.

*It is estimated that one female rabbit can produce 35 young during one breeding season. The number of young in one litter of rabbits varies from 1-9 with 4-5 being the most common. They usually leave the nest when 13-16 days of age. Source: "Missouri Conservation Agents Cook Book".*


# Crisp Fried Rabbit

2     young rabbits (about 2 lbs. each), cut into serving pieces
2     Tbs vinegar
1     tsp salt
1/2    tsp pepper
2     eggs, lightly beaten
1 1/2 Cups fine bread crumbs
2     Cups cooking oil

Put meat in a pot and cover with water. Add vinegar and boil (covered) for 15 minutes. Drain and pat pieces of meat dry. Sprinkle with the salt and pepper. Dip each piece first in egg; then in bread crumbs. Heat oil in a deep skillet until a cube of bread browns in 1 minute. Fry coated meat pieces in the hot fat until golden brown. Drain on paper towels. Place in a 250 degree oven as pieces are done and drained. Serve with Po' Folks Spiced Cabbage (page 100). and whipped potatoes.

Serves 6-8.

# Spiced Rabbit

1     cottontail rabbit (about 2 lbs.)
      bacon drippings
3     onions, coarsely chopped
2     cloves of garlic, minced (can substitute 2 Tbs garlic juice)
2     tsp paprika
1     tsp black pepper
3/4  tsp red pepper
3/4  tsp white pepper
3     bay leaves
2     tsp salt

Cut up the rabbit and saute in the bacon drippings in a deep cast iron skillet until brown. Remove and set aside.

Saute' onions and garlic in the skillet drippings and remove from the skillet. Return the rabbit to the skillet and cover with the onions and garlic . . . sprinkle with remaining ingredients. Add enough water to 2/3 cover . . . simmer, covered for 2 hours on top of the stove. Serve with (over) white rice. And, "Remember well and bear in mind, a rabbit's tail is short behind". Normally served with Honkerville Duck Salad (page 47) and Duck Camp Celery (page 101).

Serves 4.

# Hasenpfeffer
# (Spiced Hare)

| | | | | |
|---|---|---|---|---|
| 2 | cottontail rabbits or 1 snowshoe hare, cut in serving pieces | | | |
| 2 1/4 | Cups vinegar | 1/4 | tsp dried thyme |
| 2 1/4 | Cups red wine` | 2 | bay leaves, crumpled |
| 2 | Cups chopped onion | 1/2 | tsp crushed peppercorns |
| 9 | juniper berries, crushed | 1/2 | Cup vegetable oil |
| 1/2 | tsp powdered cloves | | flour |
| 2 | tsp salt | 1 | Cup sour cream |

Place the rabbit pieces and giblets in a deep ceramic bowl. Cover with a marinade made of the next 9 items. Place in the refrigerator for 24-48 hours. Turn occasionally. Drain, reserving marinade, and dry the pieces.. Roll them in flour.

Heat oil in a Dutch oven and brown the rabbit pieces. Pour off oil. Strain the marinade and add 1 1/2 cups of the strained marinade to the Dutch oven. Cover and bake in a 325 degree F oven until tender... about 1 1/2 hours. Remove the rabbit to a heated platter and keep it warm. Combine 3 Tbs flour with the sour cream and blend into the pan liquid. Cook and stir until rather evenly thickened. Pour over the meat and serve. Serve with hot biscuits.

Serves 6.

# Rabbit In Onion Sauce

| | | | |
|---|---|---|---|
| 1 | young rabbit, 2-2 1/2 pounds | 1/2 | tsp pepper |
| 2 | Tbs salt | 6 | strips fat bacon, chopped |
| 2 | quarts water | 1 | tsp salt |
| 1/2 | Cup flour | 1 | Cup sour cream, warmed |
| 1 | 10 1/2 oz. can undiluted onion soup | | |

Cut into serving pieces. Mix flour, salt and pepper together and roll meat in the mixture, coating all pieces.

In a deep heavy skillet or Dutch oven, fry the bacon until transparent and light brown. Add the meat and brown on all sides. Add the soup and sour cream. Stir and lower heat. Cover tightly and simmer for about one hour or until meat is tender, yet not falling from bones. Serve with whipped potatoes and Po' Folks Spiced Cabbage (page 100).

Serves 4.

# Squirrel Fricassee

| | |
|---|---|
| 2 | squirrels, cut in serving size pieces |
| 1 | Cup flour |
| 1 | tsp salt |
| 1/2 | tsp black pepper |
| 8 | slices fat bacon, chopped fine |
| 1 | medium onion, chopped fine |
| 4 | tsp lemon juice |
| 2 | large apples, cored, diced |
| 3 | Cups chicken broth or consomme' |

Roll the meat in the flour, salt and pepper mixture.

In a large, heavy skillet, slowly fry the bacon. Remove bacon and set aside. Turn up heat and brown the meat in the bacon fat. Sprinkle with chopped onion and lemon juice. Return bacon to skillet, add apple and chicken broth. Cover and simmer for 2-2 1/2 hours over low heat. Serve hot in a casserole with pan juices poured over. Serve with whipped potatoes, Spiced Carrots (page 99) and Corn Pudding (page 102).

Serves 4-6.

# Leftover Rabbit Salad

| | | | |
|---|---|---|---|
| 1 | Cups cooked rabbit, chopped | 1/2 | Cup sour cream |
| 1/4 | Cup French dressing | 1/2 | tsp pepper |
| 1 | Cup chopped celery | 2 | hard boiled eggs, chopped |
| 1/4 | Cup mayonnaise | | |

Mix the rabbit and French dressing in a bowl and let stand (covered) at least one hour in the refrigerator. Add rest of the stuff; mix well. Serve on lettuce lined plates.

# Fried Squirrel Cakes

| | | | |
|---|---|---|---|
| 3 | squirrels | 1 | Cup mashed potatoes |
| 1 | onion, chopped fine | 3 | Tbs bread crumbs |
| 1 | Tbs + 1 tsp tomato catsup | | bacon grease |

Parboil squirrels in salt water for 15-20 minutes. Remove meat from bones and grind coarsely. Combine ground meat with onion, catsup, potatoes and bread crumbs. Shape into cakes about 1/2" thick. Fry in the bacon grease until well browned.

# Old Baldy's Brunswick Stew

| | | | |
|---|---|---|---|
| 1 | large squirrel (old boar) | 1 1/2 | tsp salt |
| 2 | quarts boiling water | 1/2 | tsp black pepper |
| 1 | Cup whole kernel corn | 2 | 1 lb cans whole tomatos |
| 1 | Cup lima beans | 1 1/2 | tsp sugar |
| 2 | large potatoes, quartered | 1/4 | Cup butter or margarine |
| 1/2 | large onion | | |

Cut squirrel into 8 serving pieces. Bring water to boiling. Add squirrel, corn, lima beans, potatoes, onion, salt and pepper to the water. Simmer for 2 hours. Add tomatos and sugar and simmer 1 hour. Add butter and simmer about 10 minutes. Bring to a boil and remove from heat.

Serves. 4.

*Frank Rivers, longtime operator of Old Baldy's Smokehouse Bar & Billiards Emporium in Paducah, Kentucky, was a master stew developer. This squirrel concoction was one of his best.*

*A slums clearance project eliminated his place of business and . . . the Kentucky Department of Health refused to issue him a restauranteur's license at another location . . . even after he promised to bathe weekly . . . alas.*

# St. Arbor Slough Burgundy Baked Beaver

1     hind half of a young beaver, about 5 lbs.
1     Tbs sugar
      tops from a bunch of celery, tied in a bundle
1     onion, sliced
1     carrot, sliced
2     Tbs mixed pickling spices, tied in cheesecloth
1/2   tsp mint leaves, fresh or dried
1/4   Cup 5% vinegar
1     orange
2     tsp salt
3     Tbs cooking oil
      flour

Remove as much fat as possible before cooking begins. Put the meat in a large stock pot and cover with cold water. Add the next 7 items. Cut the orange in half, squeeze the juice, throw in the peels. Bring to a boil, skim and add the salt.

Reduce the heat, cover the pot lightly with foil and simmer (barely bubbling) for about 2 hours. Remove the pot from the heat and skim. Discard the spice bag, celery, orange peels and anything else that floats. Cover the pot and let it cool. Refrigerate overnight. Put a brick or something heavy on top of the meat to keep it submerged.

Come tomorrow, remove the meat and rinse it with boiling water. Drain it good. Stop up the sink with the stock. Cut the meat into chunks and sear on all sides in the cooking oil in a Dutch oven. Then, lightly dust the top of the meat with flour. Put the meat under the broiler for a few minutes to brown the flour. Remove the Dutch oven and add:

2     Tbs tomato paste mixed in 2 1/2 Cups hot beef stock
        (melt a couple bouillon cubes)
2     green peppers, cut in 5-6 pieces
1/4   tsp savory
1     Cup burgundy
      salt & pepper to taste
      dash of cayenne

Cover the Dutch oven, return to a 325 degree oven and bake for an hour. Add 2 Cups each of button mushrooms, baby carrots and small white onions. Continue baking until the vegetables are tender, about 30 minutes. Serve hot with wild or white rice.

Invite about 30 and announce the menu. The 12-15 who come will be thanking you 60 days later.

*For whatever it's worth, a beaver has valves in both his ears and nose which close when under water. It can stay under water for 15 minutes at a time. Source: "Missouri Conservation Agents Cook Book".*

# Cousin Ann's Brunswick Stew

| | | | | |
|---|---|---|---|---|
| 2-3 | Squirrels | 1 | Tbs. sugar |
| 2 | sticks butter | 1 | tsp salt |
| 1 | 15 oz. can cream style corn | 1 | tsp black pepper |
| 1 | 16 oz. can lima beans | 6 | whole cloves |
| 2 | 16 oz. cans sliced tomatos | 1/2 | tsp Worchestershire sauce |
| 4 | medium potatoes, peeled & cubed | | |

Parboil the squirrels in a large pot with enough water to cover. Remove and debone the squirrels and return to the pot along with the cooking liquid which has been strained. Add all other ingredients. Mix well and bring to a boil over medium heat. Lower heat and simmer (barely bubbling) for 2-3 hours. Sorta play it by ear . . . add water if needed.

*Cousin Ann Neely is the child bride of a good ole boy lawyer feller from Mayfield, KY She learned to cook wild game good because there wasn't much else to cook. Most of her man's early clientele were good ole boys who had trouble interpreting game laws to the letter . . . spent considerable time in jail . . . had little money to pay lawyers . . . but did have freezers full of wild meat . . ., alas. Recipes for several of Cousin Ann's creations are included for your enjoyment.*

# Roast Coon

| | |
|---|---|
| 1 | 4-6 lb raccoon, whole, all fat removed |
| 4 | large apples (greener the better), quartered |
| 2 | Cups beef, chicken or duck stock |
| 4 | wide strips fat salt pork, cut 1/4" thick |
| 4 | medium onions, peeled |
| 2 | Tbs instant minced chives |
| 2 | Tbs chopped fresh parsley |
| 1 | Tbs instant flour |

Boil the coon in salt water to cover for 30 minutes (1 Tbs salt to 1 quart water) . . . drain and pat dry and scrape the fat off (messy but not difficult).

Place apples in cavity and skewer together or sew up. Place breast side down in roasting pan. Add the stock (duck stock is best) and cover meat with the salt pork strips. Roast slowly in a 325 degree oven until tender (probably 2 1/2 hours), basting every 30 minutes with the pan juices. Place the onions in the pan during the last hour and . . . during the last half hour remove the salt pork. When done, place on a heated platter and keep warm.

Skim excess fat from pan juices and add chives, parsley and flour. Stir over medium heat until thickened and serve on the side as gravy.

Will serve 6-8 coon hunters and/or other ne'erdowells . . . 14 to 20 normal folks.

# Roast 'Possum

The best possum is a fat one taken in freezing weather, but its fat should be boiled off. Parboil the meat in salt water for about an hour and pour off and skim the fat continually. Drain entirely before roasting.

In dressing the possum, don't forget to remove the scent glands in the small of the back and beneath the front legs. The meat will be unappetizing if these are not removed. Do not skin, but dip in scalding water and pull the hairs out, then wash and scrub the skin with a stiff brush . . . like you would a hog.

| | |
|---|---|
| 1 | young 'possum |
| 2 | tsp salt |
| 4 | large red chili peppers, seeded, chopped |
| 1 | large onion |
| 6 | peppercorns, crushed |
| 8 | strips fat bacon |
| 6 | medium sweet potatoes, peeled and sliced 1/2" thick |

Put 'possum in kettle with water to cover. Add salt, red peppers, onion and peppercorns. Simmer for 30 minutes. Remove meat and place it in a roasting pan and cover with bacon strips.

Continue cooking the kettle liquid, boiling over high heat until about 2 1/2 Cups remain. Pour this over the meat and roast in a preheated 350 degree oven for 30 minutes, basting every 10 minutes. Place potatoes around the meat and continue roasting for another 30 minutes or until meat is tender and potatoes are done. It's surprisingly good. Serve with cooked turnip greens and Thunder and Lightning (page 104).

Serves 6 (invite about 30).

*Some of the good ole boy hanger ons around The Lair of The Ancient Hunter insist a 'possum needs tenderizing before cooking . . . a pick up truck does well.*

# Stewed Groundhog

| | |
|---|---|
| 1 | young groundhog, cut in 3-4 pieces |
| 1/2 | Cup vinegar |
| 2 | tsp salt |
| 2 | Tbs baking soda |
| 1 | large onion, sliced thin |
| 1/2 | tsp pepper |
| 1 | bay leaf |
| 4 | whole allspice |
| 1 | Tbs chopped fresh parsley |
| 1 | tsp Worchestershire sauce |
| 2 | tsp flour mixed with 2 tsp water |

In a large crock or ceramic (glass OK) bowl, cover meat with water and add vinegar and salt. Let stand overnight. Drain meat and put in heavy kettle. Again cover with water and add the soda. Bring to a boil and continue to boil for 20 minutes. Drain. Rinse kettle and return meat to it. Cover with water and add onion, pepper, bay leaf, allspice, parsley and Worchestershire sauce. Simmer for about one hour or until meat is tender, but not falling from bones. Put on a heated platter.

Reduce remaining liquid in kettle by boiling down to 1 1/2 Cups. Thicken with the flour mixture and pour over the meat. Serves 6. Serve with stewed tomatoes and Thunder and Lightening (page 104).

NOTE: Groundhog must have all excess fat removed as well as the kernel-like glands beneath the front legs and along the spine, 7-9 kernels in all.

*You can invite a bunch of people to partake. The 12 who don't show up will be sorry. You can substitute 2 prairie dogs for the groundhog and no one will know the difference.*

## Braised Muskrat

| | | | |
|---|---|---|---|
| 2 | 2-3 lb. muskrats | | cooking oil |
| | Bubba's Red Game Marinade (p. 90) | 1 | large tomato |
| 1 | tsp salt | | carrots |
| 1/2 | tsp black pepper | | onion |
| 1/2 | Cup flour | | celery |

Wash and dry the 'rat. Wipe it with a vinegar dampened cloth. Cut into serving size pieces. Put into a large bowl and pour the marinade over the meat. Cover and refrigerate 6 hours to overnight.

Remove meat from the marinade and drain on paper towels. Strain and reserve the marinade. Separate and reserve the carrots, onion and celery. Combine the salt, pepper and flour and dredge the muskrat pieces in it. Let them set around for 15-20 minutes.

Heat the oil in a large skillet and brown the meat on all sides. Add enough of the strained marinade to just show through the meat. Place the reserved vegetables on top. Chop and add the tomato. Bring to a boil and reduce the heat. Cover and simmer for an hour or so until the meat is tender and the liquid is much thickened. Run a spatula under the meat occasionally to keep it from sticking to the skillet. Add more marinade only if it's about to boil dry. Serve muskrat in its own sauce with fluffy white rice, mashed potatoes and hot biscuits.

Serves 6.

*General Info: Trapped animals should be taken alive from the traps and killed and dressed out within an hour. Drowning is not condusive to good meat. If the animal is frozen in the trap, I'd forget it.*

# Hoot Owl Gregory's Roast Loin Of Wild Boar

| | | | | |
|---|---|---|---|---|
| 4-5 | lb loin of young tusker | 1 | tsp salt |
| 4 | juniper berries, ground | 1/4 | tsp pepper |
| 1 1/2 | Tbs brown sugar | | dash of MSG |
| 1 1/2 | Cups apple juice | 3 | garlic cloves, slivered |
| 1 1/2 | tsp oregano | | |

Marinate 12 hours or overnight in Red Wine Marinade (page 91). Mix ground juniper berries with the brown sugar and dissolve in the apple juice. Sprinkle loin with oregano, salt, pepper and MSG. Gash the top of the loin on the fat side to a depth of 1/2" and insert the garlic slivers. Place meat on a rack in a roasting pan and roast uncovered in a 350 degree oven for 35 minutes per pound. Baste with the apple juice mixture every 15 minutes. Remove loin, spoon off all fat and make pan gravy.

Serves 12.

# Frenchy De Noux's Alligator Sauce Piquant

| | |
|---|---|
| 7 | lbs. alligator, tail preferred |
| 12 | oz. tomato paste |
| 2 | Tbs cayenne pepper |
| 3 | oz. Worcestershire sauce |
| 1/2 | Cup olive oil |
| | Tony Seasoning to taste |
| 2 | 4 oz. cans button mushrooms, drained |
| 3 | large bell peppers, chopped fine |
| 3 | bay leaves |
| 1 | 2 oz. jar Salsa de Jalapeno (hot) |
| 1 | 12 oz. can tomato sauce |
| 2 | lbs red onions, chopped |
| 2 | 10-1/2 oz. cans cream of mushroom soup |
| 1 | gal. whole tomatos |
| 2 | Tbs sweet basil |
| 3 | Tbs garlic powder |
| 1 | 6 oz. jar small green olives |
| 1 | pt. sherry |
| 1 | bunch celery, stem only, chopped |
| 1 | 4 oz. jar Pick-A-Pepper sauce |

Saute the onions, celery, bell peppers and mushrooms in the olive oil in a large skillet. Remove to a large stock pot. Now, add flour to the oil in the skillet and make a dark roux. Dump the roux into the stock pot and add the tomatos, tomato sauce and tomato paste. Stir it around a bit and add the cayenne, bay leaves, garlic powder, sweet basil and mushroom soup. Stir again, bring to a boil and turn the heat down to where the stuff just simmers along (barely bubbles) for 4 hours.

While the sauce is simmering, cut alligator meat in small cubes being sure to cut out all the tendons, gristle, etc. encountered. Fry the meat in vegetable oil until brown and place in the sauce which should have thickened by now. Add Worcestershire sauce and Pic-A-Pepper sauce and let it simmer for another hour. Add the Salsa de Jalapeno sauce. Cook until the meat is tender and falls apart. The whole operation should take 8 hours from start to finish. Wash and add the olives and cook another 10 minutes. Add the sherry. Stir. Serve over white rice.

Makes about 2 gallons . . . enough for 15-20 people.

## Border Javelina and Sauerkraut

*Javelina, when properly field dressed is quite good. To begin with, this pig has a musk sac in the middle of its back which must be cut out as soon as the animal is killed (you gotta be tough). Gutting should follow quickly and the carcass should be chilled. It should then be skinned, fat trimmed and soaked overnight in a solution of one pint vinegar to a gallon of water. Freezing may follow. Read the following recipe in its entirety before starting.*

| | | | |
|---|---|---|---|
| 3-4 | lbs Javelina meat | 1 1/2 | tsp paprika |
| 1 | large red onion, sliced | 1 | tsp lemon juice |
| 1 | large bell pepper, sliced | 3/4 | tsp salt |
| 3 | bay leaves | 3 | Cups sauerkraut, drained |
| 3 | garlic cloves, crushed | | |

Cut into chunks, place in a large pot with all the ingredients except the kraut. Cover with water, bring to a boil and lower heat. Skim and continue boiling gently until a film forms. Pour off the liquid and all that other good stuff.

Rinse the meat under hot water and start over with fresh ingredients. This time chop the onions and peppers and halve the garlic. Cook until the meat is tender and the liquid is reduced to about half. Add the sauerkraut. Heat thru and serve.

Serve 6-8.

# Waterfowl

# Little Turner Lake
# Broiled Breast of Canada Goose

| | |
|---|---|
| 1 | 6-8 pound (or thereabouts) Goose |
| 1 | Cup dry white wine |
| 1/4 | tsp freshly ground black pepper |
| 1/2 | tsp salt |
| 1/2 | tsp crumpled dry sage |
| 1 | bay leaf, crumpled |
| 1/4 | tsp chervil or marjoram |
| 1 | tsp grated onion |
| 2 | Tbs grated carrot |

Remove both breast fillets of the bird with a sharp boning knife, a fairly easy chore. Skin the fillets and place them in a bowl with mixture of all remaining ingredients. Let this mess marinate (in refrigerator, if one available) for at least eight (8) hours . . . 24 hours won't hurt. Turn every now and then so all surfaces are permeated (That means "soaked"). Drain and pat dry with old undershirt or whatever. Broil in the oven or over hot coals for eleven (11) minutes each side. Slice at an angle. Serve with Sherry Poached Apples (page 102, and When All Else Fails Baked Beans (page 96).


# Goose Breast With Orange Marmalade

*Can anyone hear the call of a flock of Canada geese without getting excited? To be in a blind when the birds respond to your call is one of the hunter's most thrilling experiences. When this roast goose is presented at the table, the thrill will be relived.*

| | |
|---|---|
| 1 | large goose breast |
| 1 | pkg. brown gravy mix |
| 1/4 | Cup flour |
| | salt |
| | sugar |
| 2 | Tbs orange marmalade |
| 1 | 6 oz. can frozen orange juice concentrate |

Preheat oven to 375 degrees. Combine all ingredients except goose breast and pour into a large glass casserole or two-inch deep roasting pan. Place meat in the pan and turn it so all sides are moistened. Cover pan tightly with aluminum foil and cook 1 1/2 to two hours or until the meat is tender. Slice the breast meat and place on a platter. Degrease pan juices and spoon over the meat. Garnish with orange slices.

Serves 4.

# Honey-Orange Roast Goose

| | | | | |
|---|---|---|---|---|
| 1 | Canada Goose | 1 | Cup orange juice |
| 4 | tsp salt | 1/2 | Cup butter |
| 2 | tsp ginger | 2 | Tbs lemon juice |
| 2 | tsp basil | 2 | Tbs grated orange rind |
| 1 | tsp pepper | 1/4 | tsp dry mustard |
| 2 | Cups honey | 2 | oranges, peeled, quartered |

Wash goose; pat dry inside and out. Put in roasting pan. Combine salt, ginger, basil and pepper. Rub this mixture inside the cavity and over skin.

Heat honey, orange juice, butter, lemon juice, grated orange rind and dry mustard . . . make a syrup of same, so to speak. Then, coat the goose cavity with 4 Tbs of this syrup. (messy). Place quartered oranges in the cavity. Then spoon 4 Tbs of the syrup over the oranges.

Truss the bird as you would a chicken, if you're handy at this thing. Pour remaining syrup over goose. Cover. Bake at 375 degrees for 2 hours. Baste with pan juices periodically. Bake, uncovered, at 325 degrees for 30 minutes.

Serve with Duck Camp Celery (page 101), long grain and wild rice prepared according to package directions, spiced carrots and the salad of your choice.

Will serve 4.

# Canada Goose Stew

| | |
|---|---|
| | meat from a goose (uncooked), cubed sorta |
| 2 | Cups peeled potatoes, coarsely chopped |
| 2 | Cups canned or frozen tomatos |
| 1 | Cup carrots, coarsely chopped |
| 1 | Cup celery, coarsely chopped |
| 1 | large onion, coarsely chopped |
| 4 | Cups tomato juice |
| 2 | Cups duck broth |
| | salt, pepper, sugar to taste |
| 1/2 | Cup flour |

Combine all ingredients except flour in a large saucepot. Cook over low heat until tender. Blend flour with a small amount of water. Stir into stew. Cook until thickened, stirring frequently.

Serves 6-8.

# Honkerville Canada Goose Breast Appetizers

2     goose breast fillets, skinned (each goose has two)
Italian salad dressing (about 1/2 bottle)
flour
cookin' oil

Slice the fillets 1/2" thick (across the grain) (short way). Cut again into 1" long pieces. Marinate the pieces in the Italian Dressing for 3-4 hours to overnight. Drain. Coat with flour. Fry in hot oil for 3-4 minutes per side. Drain on paper towels. Serve on toothpicks.

Serves 16-20. Danger of guests eating too many and not wanting your main course.

*Tastes a whole lot like deep fried chicken livers and are regularly served in the Lair of The Ancient Hunter where 25-30 Good Old Boys gather almost weekly to partake of the bounty of field and creek, and to swap lies of their expertise with rod, gun, girls, bird dogs, et al.*

# Chateau Frontenac Snow Goose

| | | | |
|---|---|---|---|
| 1 | snow or blue goose | 1/4 | Cup cream |
| 1/4 | tsp dry mustard | 1/4 | tsp pepper |
| 1/2 | Cup dry red wine | 1/4 | tsp salt |
| 1 1/2 | oz. olive oil | | flour |
| 1/2 | bay leaf | | |

Skin and remove the breast fillets and slice them at an angle into 1/4" thick steaks. Mix the wine and mustard, add the olive oil, bay leaf, salt and pepper. Place the breast slices on a flat platter or pan and pour the oily mixture over them. Let stand for 2-3 hours turning the meat occasionally.

Remove the steaks and pan fry them in their own oil over medium heat turning once. Transfer the meat to a warm platter and keep warm. Sprinkle a little flour in the skillet, stir in the remaining oil mixture, cook for 5 minutes and mix in the cream. Strain the sauce and pour over the steaks. Serve with egg noodles and glazed apple rings.

Serves 4.

# Crockpot Cherried Snow Goose

| | |
|---|---|
| 1 | Snow (or blue) goose, quartered with backbone removed |
| 1 | Tbs real butter |
| 1 | Tbs vegetable oil |
| 1 | medium onion, chopped |
| 1 | Tbs flour |
| 1 | 16 oz can sweet cherries (dark preferred) |
| 1 1/2 | Tbs cream sherry |
| 1 | Tbs light brown sugar |
| 1/2 | tsp ground cinnamon |
| 1 | beef bouillon cube melted in 1/2 cup water |
| | cornstarch |
| | salt and pepper |

Sprinkle salt and pepper liberally over the carcass and rub it in. Heat oil and butter in a skillet over medium heat and fry onion until translucent and goose quarters are golden brown. Transfer goose pieces to the crockpot and pour off all but one tablespoon of the fat in the skillet. Stir in the flour and cook for about two minutes. Meanwhile, drain the cherries, retaining 1/2 cup of juice. In a bowl, mix juice with sherry, sugar, cinnamon and bouillon. Pour the mixture into the skillet and cook, stirring constantly, until thickened. Stir in the cherries and pour over the goose. Cover and cook on low heat for 6-7 hours or until goose is quite tender.

Remove goose to a warm platter. Skim off excess grease from top of liquid left in crockpot. Dissolve cornstarch in a small amount of water and add gradually to liquid in crockpot until desired consistency is attained. Serve gravy with goose.

Serves 4.

# Barlow Bottoms Roast Duck

| | | | | |
|---|---|---|---|---|
| 4 | ducks | 1 1/2 | Cups Catsup |
| 2 | oranges, quartered | 4 | Tbs lemon juice |
| 2 | apples, quartered | 1 | grated onion |
| 4 | Tbs oil | 1 | tsp paprika |
| 4 | Tbs brown sugar | 1/2 | Cup white vinegar |
| 8 | Tbs Worchestershire sauce | | salt & pepper to taste |

Wash the ducks and wipe them dry inside and out. Then, stuff the duck cavities with the quartered fruit. Rub the said ducks with oil and place them in a baking pan. Mix the rest of the stuff in a bowl and spoon it over the ducks. Put the lid on (or cover it with aluminum foil or something) and bake at 325 degrees for two hours or until tender. Remove the lid and bake again until brown (probably 25-30 minutes). This will serve 4 of your in-laws or hunting pardners . . . and/or 8 to 12 normal law abidin' types.

*Leave out any of the prescribed ingredients and previously hidden pin feathers will sprout . . . and your mother-in-law will come for a two month visit.*

# Oven Barbequed* Duck Breasts

| | |
|---|---|
| 3 | large duck breasts (mallard, black duck, gadwall, etc.) |
| | salt |
| | paprika |
| 3/4 | Cup water |
| 3 | Tbs + 1 tsp prepared mustard |
| 2 | Tbs tomato catsup |
| 2 | Tbs Worchestershire sauce |
| 5 | Tbs butter |
| 1 | tsp paprika |
| 5 1/3 | Tbs port wine |

Build a sauce. Mix the mustard and the catsup. Add the water, Worchestershire, butter and wine. Heat this mess up over low heat. Try not to boil it.

Cut the whole breast from the ducks. Basically, this means removing the backbone. It's easy to do with a pair of kitchen shears. Imagine you're working on your mother-in-law. Now dry the breasts with a paper towel. We don't know why but all cookbook writers say to do it.

Sprinkle the breasts with salt and paprika and place on heavy duty aluminum foil in a broiler pan. Turn the edges of the foil up to form a pan within a pan. Broil the breasts (4 inches from heat) for 10 minutes. Remove from the oven and remove the fat from the foil pan. Use a turkey baster or similar suction device. Ladle some sauce over the breasts and return to the broiler for another 20 minutes basting every couple of minutes with the sauce. That's all there is to it.

Place the breasts on a heated platter and scrape the drippings into a bowl with any leftover sauce. Serve the breasts sliced thin with the sauce ladled over each slice. Breasts will be medium rare, juicy and taste great . . . too good for your wife's relatives. Now, if you want them more well done, turn the oven down to 350 and let them bake for 20 minutes. Serve with Duck Camp Celery (page 101) and Spiced Carrots (page 99).

Serves 4 to 6.

*The Good Ole Boys in Western Kentucky say it ain't barbeque, if it's cooked in an oven . . . alas . . . but for want of a better word . . .*

# Stuttgart Fried Duck Breasts

| | |
|---|---|
| 8 | duck breast fillets, boned but not skinned |
| 3 | Cups Waterfowl Marinade (see page 91) |
| 12 | strips bacon |
| 1 1/2 | Cups chopped onion |
| 4 | Tbs flour or Bisquick |
| 1 | Cup apple cider |
| 1 | Cup water |
| | salt & pepper |

Marinate the breasts in a glass or ceramic bowl in the refrigerator for 2 days. Turn occasionally. Remove the breasts from the marinade and pat dry with paper towels.

Fry the bacon until crisp in a large heavy skillet. Drain on paper towels. Drain and reserve all but 3 tablespoons of the bacon grease. Saute' the onion over low heat until translucent. Remove and set aside.

Dredge the breasts in the flour (or Bisquick) and pound some into each side of the fillets with the back of a cleaver or edge of a saucer to tenderize. Saute' the breasts over medium heat, for 4-5 minutes per side. Start with the skin side down. Remove and keep warm. Add 1 Tbs of the reserved fat to the skillet. Stir the flour into the fat in the skillet until smooth. Add the cider and water, stirring constantly until thickened and smooth. Crumble the bacon and add, along with the onion to the sauce. Season with salt and pepper to taste. Simmer for 5-6 minutes and serve with the fillets.

Serves 4. Great.

*An occasional case of pneumonia is a small price to pay for the pleasure of sitting around all day soaking wet in a cold wind with spread of duck decoys out front.*

# Honkerville Duck Salad

| | | | |
|---|---|---|---|
| 2 | Green Head Mallards | 1 | oz. of lemon juice |
| 1 | stalk celery, chopped | 1 | Cup mayonnaise |
| 8 | oz. sweet relish | | salt & pepper to taste |
| 1 | dozen hard boiled eggs, chopped | | |

Place ducks in a large saucepan with enough water to cover. Cook until very tender, drain and cool. (About 2 hours) Skin, bone and chop coarsely. Combine the chopped duck with the rest of the stuff in a large bowl and mix well. Sprinkle a few pecans on top. Refrigerate for a couple of hours. Serve with boiled possum or cold coon and collards to 10-12 village drunks.

*Honkerville is a private goose hunting club adjacent to the Ballard (Ky.) Wildlife Management Area. The Good Ole Boys at Honkerville have substituted pheasants and rabbits for the ducks in this recipe with equally good results. It is the favorite dish served at wild game dinners in The Lair of The Ancient Hunter.*

# Duck Breast Hors D' Oeuvers

2    ducks, breasts filleted and cut into bite size pieces
2    eggs, beaten
     Italian bread crumbs
3/4  Cup oil
     salt & pepper
     Ritz Crackers

Salt and pepper duck pieces to taste. Dip in egg and coat with bread crumbs. Heat oil in skillet until very hot, 375 degrees, perhaps. Fry the pieces in the hot oil until brown, turning several times. Drain on paper towels. Serve hot on Ritz Crackers.

Serves 12-16. Good . . . !

# Dabbling Duck On A Toothpick

duck breasts (skinned)        black pepper
Italian seasoning           bacon slices

Slice the duck breasts across the grain in strips about 1/2" wide. Wrap with 1/4 bacon slices (secure with toothpicks). Sprinkle with Italian seasoning and pepper. Arrange on a cookie sheet and broil on low oven rack until bacon is crisp. Drain.

Top drawer hors D' oeuvers.

# Billy Bob's Mallard Soup

2    drake mallards
2    red onions
8    stalks celery, diced
1    potato, finely diced
1    6 1/4 oz. box long grain and wild rice
     (less the seasonings)
1    oz. pkg. dry chicken noodle soup mix
1    oz. pkg. dry onion soup mix
1    oz. pkg. egg noodles

1/2  Cup barley
     salt & pepper
1/2  green pepper, diced

Put ducks in a large pot. Add two gallons of water, one sliced onion, salt and pepper. Cook for about 2 hours until duck is tender. Remove meat from bones. Return to broth which has been strained to remove scum and other awful looking stuff. Add one chopped onion, rice, the vegetables, barley and parsley. Cook at medium heat until all ingredients are tender (maybe 40 minutes). Add the soup mixes, noodles and salt and pepper to taste. Cook until the noodles are tender.

Serves 6-8.

# Chesapeake Barbequed Duck

3    Ducks, split in halves and flattened with side of a cleaver
1    lot sauce made as follows:
        Mix 1/2 lb butter, 1/2 cup tomato catsup,
        1 tsp sugar, 11/2 tsp lemon juice, 1 tsp
        Worchestershire sauce, 1 tsp black
        pepper, 1 tsp salt, 1 clove garlic
        (pressed), 1 small onion (chopped), and
        11/2 tsp Tabasco sauce. Simmer
        covered for 5 minutes.

Place flattened duck halves on a rack in a shallow baking pan. Bake at 375 degrees F for 1 hour basting with the sauce every 10 minutes. Turn and cook other side 1 hour. Continue basting.

Serves 6.

# Crockpot Eider

*Good ole boy Joe Rinella's woman has a real job down at the local meat packing house. The income from her work assures Joe a sea duck huntin' expedition to Maine every two-three years. This recipe was captured during one of these expeditions. We've substituted coots for eiders successfully... mostly because Joe's never returned with any eiders.*

6    King Eider * breasts, skinned (you always skin sea duck breasts)
3/4    Cup orange juice
1/4    Cup port wine
11/4    Tbs soy sauce
1    Tbs soy sauce
1    tsp orange rind, grated
1/2    tsp ginger
1/4    Cup honey

Marinate breasts for about two hours in salt water. Then place breasts "upright" in the crockpot. Mix all other ingredients in a separate container and pour over the breasts. Cover and cook on low heat for 8-9 hours. Don't worry about the smells that may sneak out. Results will be quite good.

Serves 6.

* *Could probably substitute Queen Eider breasts*

# Reelfoot Lake Stovetop Mallard

4     Mallard breast fillets (breasts of 2 ducks)
6     Tbs butter or margarine
2     Tbs flour
1     Cup red wine
2     Cups beef bouillon
2     small onions, sliced thin
1     bay leaf
2     whole cloves
      salt and pepper to taste
      parsley, chopped

Brown the duck breasts in the butter in a skillet. Then, transfer the duck to a heavy deep pot. Add flour to the skillet and brown it well in the butter. Gradually stir in the wine, bouillon, salt, pepper, onions, bay leaf and cloves. Bring to a boil, lower heat and simmer for 5 minutes stirring frequently. Pour this sauce over the duck breasts, cover the pot and simmer for about 1 1/2 hours or until duck is tender. If the sauce is too thin, thicken it with a little cornstarch dissolved in a small amount of cold water.

Serves 4.

# Roasted Coot

4     coots, skinned, soaked in salt water overnight
1     large potato, quartered
1     large apple, quartered
4     celery stalk tops
      salt
      pepper
12   strips of fat bacon or salt pork
1 1/2 Cups Simple Sauce Poivrade (page 90)

Wipe birds dry. Place 1/4 apple, 1/4 potato and 1 celery top in each cavity. Sprinkle birds with salt and pepper and wrap the birds with the bacon strips. Roast in 400 degree oven for 18 minutes. Remove bacon and cavity contents and serve with Simple Sauce Poivrade (page 90).

Serves 4.

# Upland Birds
# Quail To Pigeons

# Oven Barbecued Pheasant

4-5    pheasants, cut up

**Sauce:**

| | | | |
|---|---|---|---|
| 4 | sticks margarine | 6 | Tbs vinegar |
| 4 | Tbs lemon juice | 6 | Tbs tomato catsup |
| 4 | Tbs horseradish (optional) | 2 | Tbs Worcestershire sauce |
| 2 | tsp Tabasco sauce | 4 | tsp salt |

Combine all ingredients for sauce and bring to a boil. Place pheasants pieces in large shallow pan. Pour sauce over pheasant. Bake at 325 degrees for about one hour or until pheasant pulls away from the bone. About halfway during baking time, turn pieces and baste well.

Serves 12. If you're short on pheasants, substitute chuckers, . . . or broiler chickens and don't tell anyone.


# Country Fried Pheasant

| | | | |
|---|---|---|---|
| 1 | young pheasant | 4 | Tbs cooking oil |
| 1/2 | Cup flour seasoned with | 3/4 | cup red wine |
| 1 | tsp salt | 4 | Tbs flour |
| 1 | tsp black pepper | 1 1/2 | Cups cream |
| 1/8 | tsp thyme | | salt & pepper |
| 4 | Tbs butter | | |

Cut the pheasant in serving size pieces as you would a chicken. Coat with the seasoned flour.

Heat the butter and oil in a heavy skillet. Brown the pieces of pheasant on both sides over high heat. Reduce the heat, add the wine, cover and let cook for about 10 minutes. Then remove the cover and allow the bird to cook until tender. The breasts will cook faster than the legs and thighs and should be removed when they are tender and kept warm. Continue cooking the legs and thighs until tender.

Pour off all but 3 Tbs of oil, etc. from the skillet and add the flour. Blend and brown the flour and scrape up all the residue. Add the cream and cook over fairly high heat 'til the mixture thickens. Stir constantly. Season with salt and pepper and serve with the pheasant.

Serves 2 people of gentle breeding . . . one of my friends. Serve with mashed potatoes, Baked Stuffed Mushrooms (page 97), and Spicey Red Cabbage (page 100).

# Ole Craig's Spicy Pheasant

| | | | |
|---|---|---|---|
| 2 | pheasants cut in pieces | 1 | Tbs parsley flakes |
| 1 | pound Italian sausage | 1 1/2 | tsp Italian seasoning |
| 2 | Tbs butter | 1 | tsp instant chopped onion |
| 1 | 16 oz. can tomato pure'e | 1/2 | tsp salt |
| 1 | 4 oz. can button mushrooms | 1/2 | tsp pepper |
| 1 | 10 1/2 oz. can pitted ripe olives | 1/4 | tsp garlic salt |
| 1/4 | Cup liquid drained from olives | 1 | bay leaf |
| 1 1/2 | tsp celery flakes | | |

Cut sausage into bite-size pieces. Brown in a large Dutch oven. Remove sausage, pour off grease. Melt butter in the same pan. Saute pheasant pieces in the butter until brown. Remove pheasant. Add tomato pure'e to drippings and blend. Add remaining ingredients and blend. Return pheasant and sausage to the Dutch oven and spoon the sauce over same. Cover and simmer for 1 1/2 hours or until pheasant is tender.

Serves 6.

# Baked Pheasant
# From the House of Rinella

| | |
|---|---|
| 2 | pheasants cut up as you would a chicken |
| | salt & pepper to taste |
| | cooking oil, enough for browning |
| 2 | 5 oz. pkgs. chicken flavor long grain and wild rice |
| 2 | 10 3/4 oz. cans cream of chicken soup |
| 1 | 13 oz. can sliced mushrooms, drained |
| | (stems & pieces do just as well, not as pretty) |
| 3/4 | Cup sauterne, a delicate white wine |
| 1/2 | Cup sliced celery |
| 1 | Tbs chopped pimento |

Season pheasant with salt and pepper. Brown (unfloured) in the cooking oil, drain.

Prepare the rice as directed on the package (steam it). Spoon rice into a greased baking dish (9" x 14" x 2") and top with the pheasants.

Combine soup and other ingredients in a saucepan; mix well, bring to a boil and pour over the pheasants and rice. Bake, covered, at 350 degrees for 45 minutes. Uncover, bake another 15-20 minutes.

Serve with Spiced Carrots (page 99), Thunder and Lightening (page 104) and the rest of the sauterne.

Serves 6.

# Grilled Tarragon Pheasant

| | |
|---|---|
| 4 | pheasants, 2-2 1/2 pounds each |
| 1 | Cup olive oil |
| 1/4 | Cup raspberry vinegar |
| 2 | Tbs lemon juice |
| | salt & pepper to taste |
| 3 | Tbs dried tarragon or 1/2 Cup fresh, roughly chopped |
| 1 | stick butter |

Split pheasants down the middle without removing breastbones. Remove outer two portions of each wing. Marinate overnight in the olive oil, vinegar, lemon juice, salt, pepper and tarragon, turning frequently.*

Bring pheasant to room temperature (may take an hour out of refrigerator) and grill over hot coals. Baste with marinade, or preferably, melted butter. Serve with corn on the cob and Squash Casserole (page 99).

Serves 8.

*Let your woman/wife handle this phase of the work. You will need your rest.*

# Old Firehouse Barbequed Pheasant

4-5    pheasants, cut up

**Sauce:**

| | | | | |
|---|---|---|---|---|
| 4 | sticks margarine | 6 | Tbs vinegar |
| 4 | Tbs lemon juice | 6 | Tbs tomato catsup |
| 4 | Tbs horseradish | 2 | Tbs Worchestershire sauce |
| 2 | tsp Tabasco sauce | 4 | tsp salt |

Combine all ingredients for sauce and bring to a boil.

Place pheasant in a large shallow pan. Pour sauce over pheasant. Bake at 325 degrees for about one hour or until meat pulls away from bones. About halfway through the baking period, turn pheasant and baste well. Serve with Spicey Red Cabbage (page100) and mashed potatoes.

Serves 12.

# Faisan a la Creme

| | | | |
|---|---|---|---|
| 1 | pheasant | 1 | dessertspoon flour |
| 2 | oz butter | 1/2 | Cup cream |
| 2 | onions, chopped | | salt and black pepper |

Rub the butter on the inside of a casserole, put in the pheasant and the onions. Cook at 325 degrees F for an hour. Remove the pheasant and joint or carve, putting the meat onto a shallow serving dish. Liquidize the remaining liquid in the casserole; return this to the heat in a saucepan and thicken with the flour if necessary. Add the cream to the sauce and taste for seasonings. Pour over the pheasant and serve. Serve with crispy potatoes and two colourful vegetables.

Serves 4.

*This creation is the work of Good Ole Girl Jill Probert, freelance cookery columnist of Chester, Cheshire, England. She normally "hangs" her birds for 7-10 days before dressing and cooking. We were unaware of this before we had done away with three helpings and found everything wonderful.*

# Fried Quail For Breakfast

| | | | |
|---|---|---|---|
| 8 | quail | 6-9 | slices bacon |
| 1/2 | Cup flour seasoned with: | | gravy (optional) |
| 1 | tsp salt | | |
| 1 | tsp pepper | | |

Split the quail and coat with seasoned flour by shaking in a bag. Fry bacon in a cast-iron skillet and when crisp transfer to absorbent paper towels and keep warm. Fry quail in the bacon fat over medium-high heat until they are a nice golden brown on both sides. Reduce heat and continue cooking the birds until they are just tender. Transfer quail to warm platter with the bacon and serve with eggs, biscuits, gravy and boiled new potatoes.

Serves 4.

# Quail With Red Currant Jelly Sauce

| | |
|---|---|
| 8 | strips bacon |
| 10 | quail, preferably picked (woman's work) |
| 1/2 | Cup all purpose flour |
| 1 | tsp dried thyme |
| | salt & pepper |
| 1/2 | stick butter |
| 1 | large onion, chopped |
| 1/2 | Cup cream sherry |
| 1 | Tbs cornstarch |
| 2 | Cups beef stock (melt a couple bouillon cubes) |
| 1 | 11 oz. jar red currant jelly |
| 1/4 | Cup spring water |

In a big skillet or dutch oven, fry the bacon and crumble same. Reserve it. Pour off all but 3 Tbs of the fat. Wash your hands.

Now dredge the quail in the flour seasoned with the thyme, salt and pepper.

Melt the butter in the skillet with the bacon fat. Add the quail and brown on both sides . . . do it 4-5 at a time. Put them on a warm platter and set aside. Add the onions to the skillet and brown. Add sherry and boil until liquid is reduced by about half. Add stock and reduce again by half. Add jelly and cook another 3-4 minutes.

Now strain the whole mess and return the sauce to the skillet over high heat. While you're thinking about what to do next, dissolve the cornstarch in the 1/4 Cup of water and . . . add it to the boiling sauce slowly until slightly thickened. Spoon the sauce over the quail and garnish with the reserved bacon. Serve over lace potatoes or steamed long grain rice (that's the common kind found in every super market). Will serve six, if you have convinced two of them they won't like wild game.

# Lace Potatoes

| | |
|---|---|
| 3 | lbs. small potatoes, peeled and shredded |
| 1/4 | Cup cooking oil |
| 3 | Tbs butter |
| | salt & pepper |

Place the shredded potatoes in cold water to prevent darkening. Heat the oil and butter in a small frying pan. Fry about 1/3 cup at a time, flattening with a pancake turner, until sorta golden, maybe 3-4 minutes a side. Drain on paper towels. Sprinkle with salt and pepper. Repeat until potatoes are used . . . replenish oil and butter as needed. Keep warm until used.

# Tom Sutherland's Quail

8     Bob White quail
1     Cup flour seasoned with salt and pepper
      cooking oil
1     onion, chopped
1     clove garlic
3     stalks of celery, chopped fine
1     Cup white wine
1     10-1/2 oz. can cream of mushroom soup
1     Cup water

In a saucepan boil the celery until soft. Set aside. Dredge the quail in the seasoned flour and brown them in about 1/4" of cooking oil in a large cast iron pot. Remove quail and set aside. Pour off most of the oil and add celery, onion and garlic and brown until soft. Replace the quail and add the wine, soup and Cup of water, cover. Cook in 350 degree F. oven for one hour. Check occasionally and add more water if needed. Remove quail to a warm platter and set aside.

Pan drippings shall serve as a gravy. If they seem a little too thick stir in another bit of sherry. Salt and pepper to taste.

Serves 4.

*The recipe is built around 8 quail which is a one (1) day Kentucky limit and about three days bag for the author. His cooking talents are featured at his "Bayou Biltmore", a hunting type lodge on the Smithland Pool in Livingston County, Kentucky. Tom is seldom confronted with "removing the wild taste" which is not much present in pen raised birds.*

# Saddler Creek Country Style Doves

12     doves, breast or whole
3/4    Cup all purpose flour
3      chicken bouillon cubes
1/2    Cup whole milk or canned cream

1 1/2   tsp salt
1/2    black pepper
1      large onion, sliced

Salt and pepper doves to taste. Flour them and place in an oiled skillet at medium heat. Brown evenly. Remove birds and place them on a paper towel to drain. Pour excess oil from pan. Add flour to remaining skillet drippings to make gravy and stir. After paste begins to brown, add water until desired thickness is attained. Add chicken bouillon cubes to gravy. Put doves back in the pan with the gravy and top them with onions. Add the milk and stir. Cover and cook on low heat for one (1) hour.

Serves six normal souls . . . four of our personal friends.

# Fried Doves And Cream Gravy

| | | | | |
|---|---|---|---|---|
| 8 | doves (or quail) | | | salt & pepper |
| 1 | quart buttermilk | | 2/3 | Cup heavy cream |
| 1 | onion | | 2/3 | Cup milk |
| | vegetable oil | | 1/2 | Cup chicken broth |
| 1 | Cup all purpose flour + 2 Tbs | | | salt & pepper |
| 1/4 | pound bacon, cut into 1/2" pieces | | | |

Split the doves up the middle and marinate in the buttermilk for 2 hours at room temperature.

At medium heat, fry the bacon and onion in a skillet until browned and crisp. Remove the pieces and reserve. Add enough vegetable oil to the grease in the skillet to bring the depth of the combined oil to 1/4". Drain the dove halves briefly on paper towels. Mix the  Cup of flour with 1 tsp each salt and pepper and dredge the dove halves in the mixture. Shake off excess. Fry the doves a few at a time in the hot oil until golden brown . . . about 2-3 minutes per side. juices should run clear when thigh is pricked with a fork. Remove and drain on paper towels. Keep warm.

Pour off all but one tablespoon of the oil. Add the 2 Tbs of flour and stir until smooth. Add the cream, milk and chicken broth and stir until smooth. Bring to a boil stirring constantly scraping bits from the pan bottom. Lower heat and simmer for 5 minutes until thickened and smooth. Place the doves on a platter, sprinkle with the bacon and onion bits. Serve the gravy with biscuits separately.

Serves 4.

# Broiled Breast of Dove With Wild Rice

| | | | | |
|---|---|---|---|---|
| 8 | dove breasts (2 per person) | | 4 | Tbs butter |
| 1 | Cup chopped apple | | 1 | slice bacon for each breast |
| 1/2 | Cup chopped onion | | | pepper |
| 1 | tsp salt | | 1/2 | Cup sherry |

In a small sauce pan melt the butter. Add apple, onion, salt, pepper and saute' until the onion is just translucent. Remove from burner and set aside.

Wrap each dove breast with a slice of bacon using a toothpick to hold it in place. Put the breasts on a broiling rack and broil six inches from the heat source. Turn them until they are nicely browned and tender. Transfer to a casserole dish, cover with the onion-apple mixture and add the sherry. Cover and roast in a 300 degree oven for 10 minutes. Serve the breasts on a bed of wild rice mixture and accompany with broccoli.

Serves 4

# Oh Joy Smoked Doves

Doves or dove breasts, picked or skinned . . . any number.

Marinate the doves in a 50/50 mixture of pineapple juice and a cheap red wine overnight.

Wrap each dove with a half slice of bacon . . . secure with a toothpick.

Smoke three (3) hours in a "water smoker" . . . with a liberal dose of water soaked hickory chips atop the charcoal.

*Oh Joy Florence is the young wife of Good Ole Boy, Bob Florence of Calvert City, Kentucky. She became an excellent cooker of wild stuff because Bob's Good Ole Boy Buddies saw to it that his pantry was always well stocked with the bounty of field and stream . . . and his bride had little chance to cook anything else . . . was given little cash money for purchase of staples other than the essentials . . . Light Beer from Miller.*

*Bob's Good Ole Boy Buddies kept telling him that he was too good to her and if he didn't let up, she'd begin to think she was as good as he was . . . It happened. One day she announced she was going to take up hunting and fishing and accompany them on their next trip into the wilderness. The Good Ole Boys said, "Oh Joy" . . . and the name stuck.*

# South Texas Chili Doves

12    doves
12    dried chili peppers
12    slices of fat salt pork
12    slices of cold boiled ham, diced fine
1     Cup chicken broth, heated

Rub doves inside and out with salt and pepper. Place one split chili pepper in cavity of each bird. Wrap a slice of fat salt pork around each dove and secure with a toothpick.

Place birds close together in an ovenproof casserole and add the diced ham and chicken broth. Cover and bake in a 350 degree oven for 30 minutes. Remove cover and bake for another 15 minutes or until birds are thoroughly browned.

Remove the fat pork and chili peppers. Serve in the casserole with the pan juices and diced ham. Serves 4 to 6. Serve with Cheddar Cheese and Grits Casserole (page 102) and Spiced Carrots (page 99).

*Most folks find it kinda convenient to wear rubber gloves while handling the chili peppers.*

*Good Ole Boy , Joe Rinella of Southern Illinois, Southern Louisiana, Southern Texas and late of Southwestern Kentucky accumulated this recipe from some Good Ole Boys near Ozona, Texas. He done good.*

# Grandma Davis' Turtle Dove Pie

| | | | | |
|---|---|---|---|---|
| 16 | doves, whole or breast | 4 | Tbs margarine |
| 1 | onion, quartered | 4 | Tbs Flour |
| 1 | stalk celery, chopped | 1 1/2 | Cups milk |
| 4 | carrots, peeled | 3 | Tbs Madeira* |
| 1 | bay leaf | | pepper to taste |
| | salt | 1 | recipe pie crust |
| 1 | 10 oz. pkg. frozen peas, cooked, drained | | |

Combine the first five items and 1 1/2 tsp salt in a large pan with water to cover. Let it simmer for a couple of hours or whatever until doves are right tender. Bone and cut the meat into bite size pieces. Rescue the cooked carrots and chop. Strain the stock and reserve 1 1/2 cups of the stuff.

Boil the peas for 7-8 minutes as directed on the package and drain. Place the dove meat, peas and carrots in a greased 2 quart casserole.

Melt the margarine in a saucepan and blend in the flour. Add the stock and milk gradually while stirring all the time. Cook until thickened a bit, again stirring constantly. Add the Madeira and season with salt and pepper to taste. Pour the whole mess into the casserole and top with pie crust. Slit the pie crust like you've seen in the Betty Crocker ads and bake for 25-35 minutes at 425 degrees. With a little luck, it'll now be golden brown.

We've substituted duck and pheasant with equally good results. This will serve 6, if they're not allowed thirds.

*Madeira is a Portuguese white wine that costs about three times as much as general run of duck blind wines you normally drink. Try to con from a neighbor.*

# Turtle Dove Hors D'Oeuvres Supreme

| | |
|---|---|
| 12 | dove breast (Kentucky limit) (or whatever you can scrounge) |
| | salt & pepper to taste |
| 2 | eggs, beaten (Dominecker preferred) |
| | Italian bread crumbs |
| 3/4 | Cup cookin' oil (your choice) |
| | Ritz Crackers (or something similar) |

Remove the breasts with a sharp boning knife like you would those of a duck or goose. With luck you'll have 24. Salt and pepper to taste. Dip in beaten egg stuff and coat with the Italian bread crumbs. Fry in oil until brown, turning several times. Drain for a minute or two on paper towels. Serve "hot" on the crackers.

# Pepperoncinni Smoked Doves

doves, any number
pineapple juice
cheap red wine

pepperoncinni peppers
bacon slices
toothpicks

Marinate the doves overnight in 3 parts pineapple juice and 1 part cheap red wine.

Remove the doves from the marinade and place a pepperoncinni pepper atop each breast. Then wrap the dove with a bacon slice and secure it with a toothpick.

Smoke the doves in a water smoker for 1-11/2 hours. Use a full water pan (can throw in the marinade) and a half full charcoal pan.

*This is an "Oh Joy" Florence recipe and doves are served as hors d'oeuvers... For whatever it's worth, pepperoncinni peppers are green and come in a jar from the corner grocery.*

# Nebraska Roasted Chukar Partridge

| | | | | |
|---|---|---|---|---|
| 1 | chukar partridge, plucked | 1/2 | clove of garlic |
| 1 | quart milk | 1 | Tbs poultry seasoning |
| 1/4 | tsp salt | | pepper to taste |
| 1 | bay leaf | 5 | strips fat bacon |
| 1 | lemon wedge | | |

Marinate the partridge in the milk for 4-6 hours. Remove, drain and pat dry. Preheat the oven to 400 degrees. Rub the salt into the walls of the cavity of the bird. Place the bay leaf, lemon wedge and garlic in the cavity. Rub the poultry seasoning and pepper into the skin. Place the bird on a rack in a roasting pan and drape the bacon slices over the bird. Roast at 400 degrees for about 15 minutes, reduce heat to 350 degrees and continue roasting for another 50-60 minutes. When the bacon is done, remove it and baste the bird every 10-15 minutes with the drippings. The partridge will be done when the juices run clear from the thigh when it is pricked with a fork. Serve with wild rice and Swiss Broccoli Casserole (page 99).

Grouse, pheasants and prairie chickens may be prepared in the same manner.

Serves 2.

# Maine Woodcock On Toast

6 woodcocks
5 slices bacon
1 1/2 sticks butter or margarine, melted

6 slices bread
Sour Cream Sauce (page 93)
salt & pepper

Wipe dry and sprinkle birds inside and out with salt and pepper. Then, wrap each bird with bacon. Secure same with a toothpick or cotton string. Place in a buttered casserole and roast at 450 degrees for 5 minutes. Reduce heat to 325 degrees and roast for 20-25 minutes more. Remove bacon when it becomes crisp and baste frequently with the melted butter. Meanwhile, prepare the Sour Cream Sauce and reserve to pour over the birds.

Prepare the bread, which will be used as a base for the individual birds on individual plates, by removing crusts and frying until crisp in the remaining melted butter. Serve with Squash Casserole (page 99) and Spicey Red Cabbage (page 100).

Serves 6.

# Arizona Roasted Band Tail Pigeons

6 Band Tail Pigeons
6 pigeon livers (can substitute chicken livers), chopped
8 oz. button mushroom bits, and pieces, drained
3/4 Cup diced salt pork
3/4 Cup fine bread crumbs
1 Cup chicken bouillon
3 eggs, beaten lightly
3 green onions, chopped fine
1 tsp parsley flakes
6 slices bacon
1/2 Cup dry red wine
1 Tbs plus 1 tsp cornstarch
1/4 Cup cold water

Mix the chopped livers, mushroom pieces, salt pork, bread crumbs and bouillon. Press dry and mix-in the eggs, onions and parsley. Stuff the pigeons about 2/3 full of this stuff. Place in a baking pan, and cover each bird with a strip of bacon. Hold in place with toothpicks. Roast for 40-45 minutes in a 325 degree oven. Baste every now and then with the pan juices. Remove bacon about 10 minutes before removal from the oven. Hopefully, they may brown a little. Skim the grease from pan juices and add wine while stirring good. Thicken with cornstarch mixed with water. Pour over pigeons and serve hot.

Serves 6.

*Sometimes we come up a little short on Band Tails but we don't quit. We just substitute a few former residents of the belfry atop the First Methodist Church. . . Never been caught yet.*

# Grassy Lake Farms Roasted Wild Turkey

*"The Turkey is a much more respectable Bird, and withal a true original Native of America."*

*Benjamin Franklin*

1     Wild Turkey
     butter or margarine
     carrots sliced 1/4" thick
1     Cup dry white wine
     Corn Bread and Giblet Stuffing (page 94)

Bring the bird to room temperature. If it's frozen, thaw slowly in the refrigerator or other cold place. Wash the bird well inside and out. Pat dry with paper towels. Try to remove shot and bone splinters. Trim away damaged flesh.

Brush the cavity with melted butter and stuff 3/4 full with Corn Bread and Giblet Stuffing. Rub butter all over the bird . . . tuck chunks of butter in the creases under the wings and between the legs and body. Sew up and truss the bird, if you know how. Otherwise forget it and push on to next step.

Place the turkey on a bed of sliced carrots in a roasting pan. Preheat the oven to 450 degrees F. Melt 2 sticks of butter in a saucepan and add one (1) cup of wine to it. Cut a piece of cheesecloth or cotton gauze large enough to cover the bird. Soak it in the butter-wine mixture and spread it over the carcass and tuck it under. Baste again with the wine and butter. Wouldn't hurt to cover the drumsticks lightly with aluminum foil to prevent premature browning. Secure with toothpicks.

Place the turkey in the oven. Reduce heat to 350 degrees F. after 10 minutes. Baste every 30 minutes with the melted butter and wine until it runs out . . . then with the pan juices.

Roasting should require 20-25 minutes per pound. If you have a meat thermometer, insert it between the thigh and body making sure the tip doesn't touch bone before placement in the oven. Remove the bird when internal temperature reaches 190 degrees F. Don't overcook. If you can move the drumstick freely, it's done.

If the bird browns too quickly, remove the aluminum foil from the drumsticks and place a piece of foil (shiny side up) loosely over the whole bird. Remove about an hour before the roast is done. When done the bird will be brown all over and smell great. Baste from the pan and serve on a warm platter.

*Grassy Lake Farms is a commercial duck, goose and deer hunting resort on the Kentucky side of the Ohio River at its intersection with the Mississippi. Fabulous is the food served here.*

# Water Smoker Wild Turkey

*"Charcoal pan heaping full . . . plus 4-6 chunks of water soaked hickory, sassafras or grape vine . . . water pan full.*

| | |
|---|---|
| 1 | 10-16 lb. turkey |
| 1 | Tbs. salt |
| 2 | medium onions, quartered |
| 3 | stalks celery with leaves, chunked |

Rinse the turkey inside and out with cold water. Rub inside and out with the salt and place the onion quarters and celery chunks in the cavity. Place on cooking grill and smoke-cook for 10-12 hours or until turkey leg moves easily or meat thermometer reaches 180 degrees F.

Check water pan after about 4 hours cooking and bring water level back to an inch below rim with hot water.

*Variations . . . substitute Lemon & Pepper Seasoning Salt (McCormick 's) for the salt or rub some dry sage into the bird in addition to the salt. Baste the outside of the bird with honey an hour before removing to the table.*

*Smoking is slowed each time the smoker is opened . . . so "looking at the bird" should be kept to a minimum.*

# Old Poacher Filet of LBL Turkey

breast of wild turkey with skin removed
flour seasoned with salt and pepper
buttermilk
cooking oil

Remove the breast fillets (2) from the carcas with a sharp boning knife.Slice the fillets about 3/8" thick (across the grain). Cut again into 2" long pieces. Marinate the pieces in buttermilk for 2-3 hours. Remove them and roll in the seasoned flour.

Fry in 1/2" hot cooking oil until brown . . . about 3-4 minutes per side turning once. Drain on paper towels and serve as hors d' oeuvers . . .

*This is great stuff. Better stash a few pieces for yourself before placing it on a table before the wolf pack.*

# Frances MacIlquhan's Blackbird Pie

4 & 20 blackbirds, picked or skinned, split and cleaned
1/2    Cup vinegar
1/4    tsp mace
1      lemon, juice and grated rind
1/4    tsp sugar
1      onion, stuck with 2 cloves
       dry red wine or claret
1      pastry for 2-crust 12" pie
3      Tbs butter
       flour
       salt and pepper
1      pinch nutmeg
       milk

Marinate the dressed birds in water and the vinegar for 2-3 hours. Drain, rinse and put them into a deep pot. Barely cover with water and add the mace, lemon juice, half of the grated rind and the sugar. Bury the onion in the meat. Bring to a boil, skim and reduce the heat. Simmer until the meat is ready to fall from the bones, adding wine to keep the birds covered with liquid. Take out and remove the breasts intact and smaller bits of meat. Save the liquid.

Line a 12" round baking dish with pie crust dough and add the meat. Preheat the oven to 425 degrees F. Boil the reserved liquid until about 2 Cups are left. Throw the onion away. Rub the butter in flour using as much flour as necessary to make a mealy mixture. Sprinkle this butter-flour mixture over top of the boiling liquid. Stir until blended and thickened. Add salt and pepper to taste and the nutmeg.

Pour the sauce over the meat. Cover with pastry. Pinch the edges of both crusts together and brush with milk. Score and bake in the now hot oven for 10 minutes. Reduce heat to 375 degrees F and bake for about 45 minutes, or until the pie is evenly browned all over. A glass "pie dish" allows you to tell if the bottom is browning.

Serves 10-12.

# Good Times &
# Good Ole Boys

*Hog feeding time in the Lair of the Ancient Hunter. Female at lower right was uninvited guest . . . showed up unannounced trying to catch her man having fun with another woman. Now, other good ole boys present are in deep trouble because their women have heard the woman was there.*

*You ain't going to believe this but . . .*

*Investment Club meeting.*

*A pair of deuces makes for excellent investment portfolio . . . when backed up with a 38 . . . profit taking in order.*

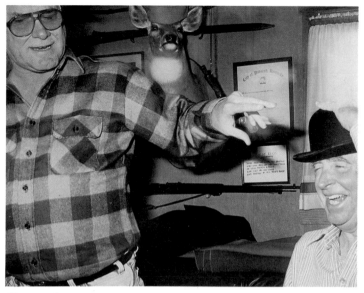

*Watermellon wasn't on the menu but it looks like Good Ole Boy at the left just ate one. Marquis of Chittingham at right always dresses formally for dinner.*

*They say, "Lean may be in but fats where it's at." It's obvious that two of these good ole boys have little fear of saturated fats and cholesterol.*

*31st Street Philosophical and Cut Bait Society members keep fit with daily calisthenics.*

*Ooops! Introduction of personal equipment has been known to be hazardous to shooters health.*

*Most of the Lair's kitchen volunteers wear XXL shirts.*

*Heavy duty kitchen duty.*

*Don't have to label this photo to know it cantains a Good Ole Boy.*

*A sky full of blues and snows in Ballard County, Kentucky.*

*Style show following the hunt. Geese are props. For a dollar you get your picture taken.*

*The most intelligent fellow in the hunting party.*

*It's tough work but somebody's got to do it.*

*Decoying Canadas about to become table fare.*

*I'll be a Good Ole Boy, if you'll just let me outta here.*

*A matched pair. Every Good Ole Boy needs one.*

*Canadas decoy easier the day after the season ends.*

*The best way to keep your woman happy is to make her feel she's an integral part of your world. Keep her busy . . . have a few chores laid out for her when she gets home from her regular job.*

# Fish & Other
# Water Critters

# The Lair's Fried Catfish

10-12 lbs catfish (crappie, bass, bluegills do equally well)
        cooking oil
1 1/2 Cups milk
1      Cup plain flour
2 1/2 Cups white cornmeal
1 1/2 tsp ground red pepper
1      Tbs salt
1      Tbs paprika
1      tsp garlic powder
4      Tbs barbeque sauce (optional)

Mix the dry ingredients real good in a bowl or bag. Dip the fish in the milk; then in the dry mixture*. Deep fry in 350-375 degree F cooking oil deep enough to float the fish. Remove the fish when it browns and floats to the top. Barbeque sauce can be added a little at a time as the frying proceeds. You'll be glad you did... careful though it'll cause the oil to "boil up".

Most good ole boys will eat a pound of fish with bones in them-.., 1/2 to 3/4 pound of fillets.

*Dry ingredients are mixed in "doubled" brown super market bags in the Lair of the Ancient Hunter. Fish pieces are added and given a good shaking. It coats them good.*


# Pine Bark Stew

4      lbs Bream (bluegills), scaled, beheaded and gutted
1/2    lb salt pork, sliced thin
3      6 oz cans tomato paste
6      oz tomato catsup
4      large onions, chopped coarse
1      tsp red pepper
2      tsp salt

Place fish in 8 quart pot and barely cover with water. meanwhile, fry the salt pork in a skillet until most of the fat is rendered. Remove the pork and drain on paper towels. Drain off all but a tablespoon of the fat. Saute the onions in this until translucent. Now, pour the onions into the big pot atop the fish and follow with the tomato paste and tomato catsup. Do not stir... just leave sorta layered. Sprinkle the salt and pepper over the whole mess and bring to a medium boil... Cook for 20-30 minutes. Serve with white rice.

Serves 8-12.

*Oh Joy Florence sweet talked this recipe out of an ancient Columbia, South Carolina lawyer. Supposed to be top drawer stuff.*

# Bubba's Fish Stew

| | |
|---|---|
| 2 | lbs. white meat fish fillets (fresh or salt water) |
| 1 | medium onion, chopped |
| 1 | Tbs tabasco sauce |
| 2 | Tbs cooking oil |
| 2 | 10-3/4 oz cans cream of potato soup |
| 2 | cups milk |
| 1 | 16 oz can stewed tomatoes, undrained |
| 1 | 10 oz package frozen mixed vegetables, thawed |
| 1 | 8 oz can whole kernel corn, drained |
| 1 | tsp salt |
| 1/2 | tsp pepper |

Saute the onion in oil in the stew pot until translucent. Add all other ingredients except the fish and heat, stirring occasionally until the stew is simmering.

Cut fish fillets into 1 inch chunks and add to the pot. Continue to simmer for another 10-15 minutes until the fish is done.

Serves 6.

# Shirley's Fish Dip

| | |
|---|---|
| 1 | Cup cooked fish, flaked or mashed |
| 2 | ripe avocados, peeled and mashed (save seeds) |
| 2 | Tbs lemon juice |
| 2 | tomatoes, chopped |
| 1/4 | Cup mayonnaise |
| 1/4 | Cup onions, minced |
| 2 | cloves garlic, minced |
| 1/2 | tsp Tabasco |
| | salt and pepper to taste |

Mash the avocados in a bowl and sprinkle with lemon juice. Add all other ingredients ( including seeds) and mix well. Cover and place in refrigerator for an hour or two before serving as a dip for chips or crackers.

*Women are to blame for most of the lying fishermen do. They insist on asking questions.*

# Fish Stock

| | |
|---|---|
| 3 | pounds fish trimmings (heads, tails, fins) |
| 2 | Tbs butter |
| 2 | carrots, sliced |
| 2 | onions, sliced |
| 2 | stalks celery with leaves, sliced |
| 6 | sprigs parsley |
| 1/4 | tsp thyme |
| 1 | tsp garlic juice |
| | salt and pepper to taste |
| 6 | peppercorns |
| 1 1/2 | Cups red wine |
| | Water to cover |

Combine all ingredients in a large soup pot. Partially cover and bring to a boil slowly; reduce heat and simmer for 30 minutes. Strain stock into a bowl.

# Friday Fish Chowder

| | |
|---|---|
| 2 1/2 | lbs white-meat fish fillets (fresh or salt water) |
| 1/4 | Cup dry red wine |
| 1 | tsp dried thyme |
| 2 | whole cloves |
| 1/2 | tsp salt |
| 1 | small onion, thinly sliced |
| 1/2 | Cup carrots, chopped |
| 1/2 | Cup celery, chopped |
| 1/2 | green pepper, chopped fine |
| 1 1/2 | Cups fish stock (page 82) |
| 1 | Tbs butter |
| 2 | Cups heavy cream |

Cut fish into 11/2 inch pieces. Cover half of the pieces with the wine and set aside for 30 minutes.

Meanwhile, in a soup pot, put the herbs, seasonings and vegetables in the fish stock, and simmer until the vegetables are tender.

Remove the pieces of fish from the wine, and combine them with the other fish pieces. Now, saute them in the butter in a small skillet for about 5 minutes. Remove the fish from the skillet and add to the pot with the vegetables. Cook over medium heat until the fish pieces are done... probably 6-8 minutes. Scald the cream and add it to the pot. Stir and serve.

Serves 6.

# Hot Salmon Salad Sandwiches

8     oz cooked salmon
      or
1     8 oz can canned salmon

9     hard boiled eggs, chopped
1     Tbs chopped green pepper
2     Tbs chopped onion
2     Tbs sweet pickle relish
1/2   Cup mayonnaise on salad dressing
8     hamburger buns

Mix all ingredients. Split buns and fill with mixed ingredients. Wrap in foil and bake in oven at 250 degrees for 25-30 minutes.

Serves 8.

# Poached Salmon

1     5-7 lb whole fish, dressed with head  removed
      Court bouillon (see page 84)

*Large fish require a large fish kettle. Most any deep vessel will do, a large stock pot, deep roasting pan or copper boiler,  perhaps. We use a 26 inch long "fish poacher" which has an internal perforated rack upon which the fish can be lowered or raised into or out of the court bouillon. It is important for the fish to be fully covered. If necessary, add water to accomplish this. If a vessel other than  a fish poacher is used, the fish should be tied in wet cheese-cloth (dipped in court bouillon) leaving tabs long enough to hang outside the pot for easy handling.*

Prepare the court bouillon as directed.   Meanwhile rinse the fish under running cold water and place it on the poaching rack; lower into the liquid and simmer (not quite a boil) for 10 minutes per inch of fish thickness at its thickest part. Remove rack from the poacher and with 2 pancake turners,  place fish on a large platter.  Remove and discard the skin from the top side of the fish.

In the Lair of the Ancient Hunter we usually serve the salmon "hot" with a Hollandaise Sauce.  It can be refrigerated, garnished with lemon slices and parsley and served with Herb Mayonnaise.

Serves 6-10.

# Court Bouillon

| 12 | Cups water | 3 | bay leaves |
|----|-----------|---|-----------|
| 3 | carrots, peeled and quartered | 1 | tsp parsley flakes |
| 2 | onions, sliced about 1/4" thick | 15 | peppercorns |
| 6 | green onions or scallions | | Juice of 3 lemons |
| 3/8 | tsp thyme | | |

Combine all ingredients except lemon juice.
Bring to a boil. Lower heat to simmer. Cover pot and cook 30 minutes. Strain and add lemon juice.

*Court bouillon is a "shortly boiled "aromatic liquid in which fish and shellfish are cooked.*

*Court bouillon is usually made in the vessel in which the fish is to be cooked. It is not a fish stock and is usually discarded following its use.*

# About Fish Tales

*Small mouth bass are known to lie in shady spots. Rainbow trout, on the other hand, often lie in bright sunshine. Fishermen, in general, are never fussy where they lie. Listen for them around your favorite watering hole*

# Buttermilk Fried Crappie

| 2 | lbs crappie or bass fillets |
|----|-----------|
| 1/2 | Cup buttermilk |
| 1/2 to 1 | Cup oil |
| 1/2 | Cup cornmeal, fine ground preferred |
| 1/4 | tsp cayenne |
| 1/2 | tsp paprika |

Cut the fillets into serving-size pieces. Place in a shallow bowl and cover with the buttermilk. Let them marinate for 15-30 minutes., In the meantime, mix the cornmeal, salt, pepper, and cayenne together. Remove the fillets letting excess buttermilk drip off. Drop them into the cornmeal mixture; coat well.

Slowly heat the oil to 375 degrees F; put the fish into the skillet (don't crowd) and fry on both sides until golden brown and cooked... probably 4-5 minutes per side. Drain. Serve hot.

Serves 4.

# Pore Boy Shrimp Hors d'Oeuvers

12-15 Hand size bluegills (or a bucket of little ones)
1      Tbs Shrimp Boil
2      qts water
1      tsp salt
1      bowl crushed ice
       toothpicks
       wire basket

Scale and fillet the bluegill and cut into chunks about 3/4 inch wide.

In a deep pot, bring water, Shrimp Boil and salt to a rolling boil.

Place 8-10 of the fillets in a wire basket and lower it into the boiling water. Boil for 8-10 seconds or until the fish turn white and "blossom". Remove and dump the fillets into, onto, over (whatever) a bowl of crushed ice.

When fillets are cold impale them on toothpicks and serve with your favorite shrimp dip. Fifteen big bluegills should make 50-60 hors d'oeuvers. Blindfolded you'll think you're eating shrimp and they're considerably cheaper. Even your woman can catch a bluegill every now and then.

*These delicacies are served often in The Lair of the Ancient Hunter ... most every time someone gives us a mess of bluegills.*

# Old John's Broiled Bass Fillets

4      good sized bass fillets          1      Tbs lemon juice
1/2    stick butter                            salt
1      Tbs soy sauce                           pepper
1      tsp garlic powder

Salt and pepper the fillets (both sides) and place in broiler pan and baste with a sauce made from the melted butter, soy sauce, garlic powder and lemon juice. Broil for 4 minutes, turn, baste with the butter sauce and broil another 4 minutes.

Serve on a heated plate with what's left of the butter sauce. Dip bite size pieces into the sauce as you gorge.

Serves 2.

*A Texan caught a bass that weighed 8 pounds. Texas style, he told Old John his Kentucky guide, that in Texas they used that kind for bait. Old John nodded, threw it back.*

# Saucy Baked Bass or Crappies

3 1/2 pounds bass or crappie fillets
1 Cup cornbread mix
1/2 Cup flour
1 Tbs seasoned salt
1 Cup cooking oil
1/2 bell pepper, chopped

1/2 onion, chopped
1 can tomato soup
1/2 soup can water
salt
pepper

Salt and pepper the fillets (both sides) and bread them in a mixture of the cornbread mix, flour and seasoned salt. Fry (brown) fast in the cooking oil. Remove from oil and drain on paper towels. In the meantime, saute the bell pepper and chopped onion in a Dutch oven until soft. Pour off the oil and add the soup and water. Bring to a boil and remove from the stove. Add the browned fillets and bake, uncovered in a preheated 375 degrees F oven for 10-15 minutes. Remove fillets to warm plates, cover with sauce and serve.

Serves 4.

# Pressure Canned
# Ohio Valley Salmon or Tuna
## (Carp, Buffalo, White Perch)

Clean the carp by filleting the meat from the bones and skin the best you can. Cut the fillets into 1 1/2" to 2" cubes. Pack meat into sterile pint or quart jars to 1/2" of top. Add 1 tsp vinegar and 1/4 tsp salt to each pint jar . . . double this for quarts. Process in a pressure cooker for 100 minutes at 10 pounds pressure. The canned fish will be pink and can be used in any recipe calling for salmon or tuna. Guests will never know the difference if you do not spill the beans.

# Charcoal Grilled Trout

Trout-number available with heads and skin left intact
vegetable oil
melted butter
lemon juice
salt and pepper

Cover charcoal grill with aluminum foil and lightly oil it with vegetable oil. Coat inside of each trout with melted butter and lemon juice. Salt and pepper liberally. Grill for 7-8 minutes on one side. Turn and repeat for other side. When fish is turned, skin will peel off. Brush exposed side with the butter and lemon juice. Serve hot.

# Broiled Halibut Steak With Eggplant Sauce

2     large green peppers
1     large onion
1     1 lb. eggplant
2/3     Cup vegetable oil
2     15 oz. cans tomato sauce
2/3     Cup white wine (dry)
2     garlic cloves, minced or 2 Tbs prepared garlic juice
       (like you buy in a bottle)
1     bay leaf
1/2     Cup butter
4     Tbs lemon juice
1     tsp salt
1/2     tsp pepper
3 1/2-4 lbs. halibut steak

Cut the green peppers into 1/2" wide strips and thinly slice the onion. Peel the eggplant and cut it into 1/2" cubes. In a 12" skillet or dutch oven over medium heat in hot oil, cook the green pepper and onion until tender; then add the cubed eggplant. Let this cook (while stirring) about five minutes then add the tomato sauce, wine, bay leaf and garlic. Simmer for another 15 minutes "covered".

While all this is going on, grease the broiling pan rack with the butter and . . . in a one quart saucepan over low heat, melt the butter with the lemon juice, salt and pepper. Place the halibut steak(s) on the rack and brush generously with the butter mixture. Broil 5-6 minutes and turn. Brush again with the butter mixture. Broil 5 minutes longer or until the fish flakes when tested with a fork. Serve the steak(s) with the hot eggplant sauce.

*This combination of halibut and sauce is kinda expensive. Serve only to people you really want to impress, like a new girl friend. Don't waste on relatives or hunting and fishing friends.*

# Fried Fish Patties

1     qt. canned carp (page 86)        1/2     tsp black pepper
1     Tbs and 2 tsp lemon juice                 crushed cracker crumbs
2     eggs, beaten lightly                       vegetable oil

Mix first four items plus enough cracker crumbs to make the mixture of a consistency to form firm patties. Fry in hot vegetable oil until brown. Turn once.

Will make 8 patties. Tell guests they're salmon.

# Fried Snapping Turtle

*A turtle has both white and dark meat. Great meat is found in the legs, neck, tail and a small tenderloin like thing against the shell.*

Cut into pieces about 2" long and tenderize with the back side of a meat cleaver. Salt and pepper to taste; dredge in flour and fry in about 1" of vegetable oil over low to medium heat . . . (covered) until tender and brown. Failure to cover the skillet may allow the turtle to crawl out.

*Dressing the turtle may be your woman's toughest assignment to date. She'll need a hatchet, some catfish skinning pliers and a sharp knife or two. Good ole boy, Gene Lindsey of Lewis County, Missouri says he can dress one in 10-15 minutes. Your woman may need an hour or two for her first one.*

# Frog Pond Lobster Hors d' Oeuvers
## (Crayfish)

1/2   gallon (or more) deveined crayfish tails
1     gallon water
1     Tbs salt
1     3 oz. bag Crab and Shrimp Boil

Bring water to a boil in a large pot and add salt and Crab and Shrimp Boil. When water has returned to a boil, add the crayfish tails. Leave on heat for about 5 minutes (crayfish should be pink in color). Remove from heat and drain. Cool crayfish by placing them atop a large bowl of crushed ice. Serve with your favorite shrimp dip. You'll be a hero.

# Marinades, Sauces & Stuffings

# Simple Sauce Poivrade

1     Tbs + 1 tsp butter or margarine
2     shallots, chopped
1/4  tsp black pepper
1     Tbs lemon juice
1     Cup bouillon or pan drippings with fat skimmed off
      black pepper

Melt butter in a saucepan and saute' shallots until golden. Season with pepper to taste. Add lemon juice and bouillon or pan drippings plus enough stock to make two cups of liquid.

Boil over high heat until sauce is reduced to about 1 1/2 cups.


# Bubba's Red Game Marinade

1     Cup beer
1     Cup dry red wine
1     bay leaf
8-10 peppercorns
1     onion, sliced
1     tsp crushed dried rosemary
1     clove garlic, minced
1     stalk celery with leaves, quartered
1     carrot, quartered

Mix the ingredients in a ceramic or glass container.

Marinate the steaks or chops for 2-3 hours at room temperature or 4-6 hours in the refrigerator. Yield: 2 1/2 cups—enough for 2-3 pounds game sliced 1" thick.


# Venison Marinade

1     Cup vinegar
1/2  tsp dried sage
1/2  tsp thyme
1     tsp dried mint or 1 Tbs chopped fresh mint
2     Tbs minced onion
2     Cups olive or vegetable oil

Soak the herbs and onion in the vinegar overnight. Combine the mixture with the oil and pour over the venison, turning to coat all sides. Cover and allow to marinate overnight or longer, depending on toughness and age of meat.

Makes 3 cups.

# Red Wine Marinade

| | | | |
|---|---|---|---|
| 1 1/2 | Cups vegetable oil | 1 | bay leaf |
| 1 | large stalk of celery, chopped | 8 | peppercorns |
| 1/2 | Cup onion, finely chopped | 8 | juniper berries, crushed |
| 1 | clove garlic, minced | 1 | pinch thyme |
| 1 | shallot, minced | 1 | pinch rosemary |
| 1 | large carrot, sliced thin | 3 1/2 | Cups cheap red wine |
| 1 | Tbs fresh parsley, minced | | |

Heat 1/4 cup of the oil in a large skillet or Dutch oven. Add and saute' the vegetables, spices and herbs until the onions are clear and golden. Remove from heat and stir in remaining oil and wine. Cool and pour over meat.

Makes enough for about 5 pounds of bear, venison, elk, antelope, moose, etc.

# Waterfowl Marinade

| | | | |
|---|---|---|---|
| 1 | onion, sliced | 1 | carrot, sliced |
| 2 | cloves garlic, minced | 1/2 | tsp salt |
| 1 | bay leaf | 1/2 | tsp black pepper |
| 2 | stalks celery with leaves, sliced | | |

In a glass or ceramic container mix the ingredients. Marinate bird for 2 days, refrigerated. Yield: 3 cups-enough for 4 duck breasts, 2 ducks or 1 goose.

# Rib and Fowl Bar-B-Que Sauce

| | |
|---|---|
| 2 | Tbs brown sugar |
| 2 | cloves garlic, minced |
| 1 1/2 | tsp paprika |
| 1 | tsp pepper |
| 1 1/2 | tsp salt |
| 1 | onion, minced |
| 2/3 | Cup catsup |
| 2/3 | Cup tomato juice (can use pineapple juice) |
| 1 1/4 | Cups water |
| 1 | Cup cider or white vinegar |
| 1 | Tbs Worcestershire sauce |
| 1/4 | Cup vegetable oil |

Bring all ingredients to a boil in a medium sized pot. Reduce heat and simmer uncovered 20 minutes. Store in container with tight lid and refrigerate between uses.

Makes about 5 cups.

# Cider Barbecue Sauce

| | | | | |
|---|---|---|---|---|
| 1 | clove garlic, minced | 2 | tsp celery seed |
| 1 | Cup cider | 2 | tsp chili powder |
| 1 | Cup ketchup | 2 | Tbs Worcestershire |
| 1 | Tbs brown sugar | 5 | drops Tabasco |
| 1 | tsp dry mustard | | |

Stir all ingredients in a saucepan. Bring to a boil. Reduce heat and simmer uncovered 30 minutes. Baste turkey, brisket, game or ribs.

Makes 2-1/4 cups.

# Herb Mayonaise

| | | | | |
|---|---|---|---|---|
| 1 1/2 | Cups mayonaise | 1 | tsp tarragon |
| 1/2 | Cup chopped parsley | 1 | tsp chervil |
| 1/2 | Cup chopped watercress | 1/2 | tsp salt |
| 1/4 | Cup chopped chives | 1/2 | tsp pepper |

Blend (in covered blender) all ingredients until well mixed and green. Cover and refrigerate until serving time.

# Ole John Skellion's Bar-B-Que Sauce

| | | | | |
|---|---|---|---|---|
| 32 | oz. tomato catsup | 1 | 12 oz. bottle Tabasco |
| 32 | oz. tomato juice (or sauce) | 4 | garlic buds (optional) |
| 1 | Cup Worcestershire sauce | 3 | Cups vinegar |
| 1 | Cup vegetable oil | | salt and pepper to taste |

Combine ingredients and bring to a boil. Reduce heat and simmer (with lid off) for one (1) hour. Store in a tight lidded container. Does not require refrigeration.

*There are many World Champion grade open pit barbequers among the Good Ole Boys in far Western Kentucky. These Boys know your body craves energy in large quantities while you're firing a pit. They are firm believers that "protein alone" is not enough to provide this energy. They're unimpressed with all the medical gobbledegook about the evils of fats and sugars. They know full well that alcohol converts to rich body sugar and . . . one must keep his strength up!"*

*All the Good Ole Boys agree that Ole John Skellion makes a mean sauce. It took three (3) sittings to get the recipe on paper. He just didn't remember it the same every time . . . something to do with his rich blood sugar count . . . probably.*

# 808 Barbeque Sauce

| | | | | |
|---|---|---|---|---|
| 2 | qts. water | 4 | Tbs black pepper |
| 1 | Cup vinegar | 2 | Tbs cayenne pepper |
| 4 | Tbs butter or margarine | 2 | cloves garlic, finely chopped |
| 1 | tsp sugar | 2 | Tbs Worcestershire |

Slop it all together and boil it about 4 minutes. Add a bit of cornstarch, if you wish to thicken. Refrigerate between uses.

*Ruth Barnes was an entertainer of sorts who operated an establishment "primarily" for the enjoyment of male hunters and fishers at 808 Washington Street in Paducah, Kentucky, for many years. She was ever in the front of those who would preserve wildlife. She was also an excellent cook of wild critters and several of her best works are included herein.*


# Lydia Shelterdove's Barbecue Sauce

| | | | | |
|---|---|---|---|---|
| 1 1/2 | tsp salt | 2/3 | Cup ketchup |
| 1 | tsp pepper | 2/3 | Cup tomato or pineapple juice |
| 1 1/2 | tsp paprika | 1 1/4 | Cups water |
| 2 | Tbs brown sugar | 1 | Cup cider or white vinegar |
| 2 | cloves garlic, minced | 1 | Tbs Worcestershire |
| 1 | onion, minced | 1/4 | Cup vegetable oil |

Boil all ingredients in a medium-sized pot. Reduce heat and simmer 20 minutes. Transport sauce in a plastic tub closed with a tight-fitting lid. At the barbecue, transfer sauce to a stainless steel dish and keep warm on top of the grill.

Makes about 5 cups.


# Sour Cream Sauce

| | | | | |
|---|---|---|---|---|
| 2 | Tbs dry white wine | 1/2 | Cup sour cream |
| 1 | tsp lemon juice | 1 egg yolk | |
| 2 | Tbs chopped green onion | | |
| 1 | tsp chopped parsley | | |
| 1/4 | tsp dry tarragon | | |

Combine the wine, lemon juice, onion, parsley and tarragon in a small saucepan. Bring to a boil and let boil until the liquid is reduced by about one half . . . probably 4-5 minutes. Blend the sour cream and egg yolk in a bowl. Slowly add the wine mixture stirring as it is added. Return to the saucepan and simmer over low heat for 3-4 minutes. Do not boil.

# Corn Bread and Giblet Stuffing

1        Cup celery, chopped
1        Cup onion, chopped
1/4      Cup butter or margarine
4        Cups corn bread, crumbled
4        Cups stale white bread, cut in small cubes
1        Cup turkey or chicken giblets, cooked and chopped
1        tsp salt
1/2      tsp poultry seasoning
1/4      tsp black pepper
1        egg
1 3/4 Cups water

Saute the celery and onion in the butter until translucent. Add the corn bread and stale bread. Cook, stirring until light brown. In a saucepan warm the water a bit and add the salt, pepper, poultry seasoning and egg. Stir up and pour over the stuffing, mixing good. Now, stuff the wild turkey.

Makes about 6 cups.

# Chestnut Stuffing

| | | | | |
|---|---|---|---|---|
| 1-1/2 | pounds chestnuts | | 2 | tsp salt |
| | water | | 1 | tsp thyme |
| 1/4 | pound butter | | 1 | tsp savory |
| 1-1/2 | Cups celery, diced | | 1/2 | tsp pepper |
| 1 | Cup onions, chopped | | 8 | Cups fresh bread crumbs |

Score the chestnuts across the bottom of the shell with a sharp knife. In a large saucepan, cover chestnuts with water and over high heat, bring to boiling; cook one minute and remove from heat. With a slotted spoon remove a few chestnuts at a time; remove shells and skins and chop coarsely.

In a Dutch oven over medium heat, melt butter and cook celery and next 5 ingredients about 10 minutes or until vegetables are tender. Remove from heat, add chopped chestnuts and bread crumbs. Mix well.

Makes 10 cups.

*Since native American chestnuts are almost non-existent, you may substitute Chinese Chestnuts or other nursery varieties and none will know.*

# Game
# Accompaniments

# When All Else Fails Baked Beans

| | | | |
|---|---|---|---|
| 1 | pound can of pork and beans | 8 | bacon strips, cut in 1" lengths |
| 1 | can kidney or pinto beans | 1 | clove of garlic, minced |
| 1 | can cut-up green beans, drained | 1 | onion, chopped |
| 1 | can lima beans, drained | 1 | Cup brown sugar, packed |
| 1 | can wax beans, drained | 1/2 | Cup vinegar |
| 1 | can garbanzo beans | 1 | tsp dried mustard |

Dump all the beans in a Dutch oven and stir them up. Saute the cut-up bacon in a large skillet along with the minced clove of garlic and chopped onion. When these are golden soft, add the sugar and dry mustard. Stir a bit. Pour this sauce over the beans and bake in a 350 degree oven for an hour and 9 minutes or thereabouts.

Serves 12-16.

*These beans appear frequently on the menu in the Lair of the Ancient Hunter. Everything can be done a day ahead except the final baking. If more Good Ole Buddies show up than are invited, you can thrown in another can of beans, whatever's handy. If there are leftovers, you may warm them 2-3 times and serve to your woman's relatives.*

# Red Beans And Rice

| | | | |
|---|---|---|---|
| 2 | Cups dried kidney beans | 1 | pod garlic |
| 2 1/2 | quarts water | 1 | bay leaf |
| 3 | Tbs shortening or bacon fat | 2 | Tbs chopped parsley |
| 1 | large onion, chopped | 1 1/2 | Cups uncooked rice |
| 1 | small green pepper, chopped | | salt & pepper |
| 1/4 | lb. salt pork (or ham bone) | | |

Soak beans in water overnight. Melt fat in iron pot and saute' onion and green pepper. Add beans, and soaking water plus enough additional water to make 2 1/2 quarts, pork (or ham bone), garlic and bay leaf. Simmer slowly 3-4 hours or until creamy. Season to taste, add parsley; serve over hot cooked rice.

Serves 6.

# French Fried Onion Rings

| | | | |
|---|---|---|---|
| 3 | large onions, sliced 1/4" thick | 1 | Cup flour |
| | salad oil | 1/2 | tsp salt |
| 1/2 | Cup milk | | |

Separate the onion slices into rings. Heat 1/2" to 3/4" salad oil in a deep skillet. An electric skillet is ideal and 370 degrees is the best temperature.

Place the milk in a small bowl. In another bowl mix the flour and salt. Dip onion rings in the milk, then in the flour-salt mixture. Repeat the process to coat twice. Cook the rings in the hot oil until lightly browned . . . about 3 minutes. Drain on paper towels . . . serve immediately.

## Green Pea Casserole

| | |
|---|---|
| 2 | cans (16-17 oz. net wt.) of peas, drained |
| 2 | 10 3/4 oz. cans cream of mushroom soup |
| 1 | Cup (8 oz.) sour cream |
| 1/2 | tsp salt |
| 1/4 | tsp garlic salt |
| 1 | Cup cracker crumbs |
| 1 | Cup shredded cheddar cheese |
| 1/2 | Cup melted butter (1 stick) |
| 2 | medium onions, French fried |

Mix soup, sour cream, salt and garlic salt together. Stir in peas. Pour into greased or sprayed 8" x 12" baking dish. Top with cracker crumbs . . . then cheddar cheese. Pour melted butter over all. Bake uncovered at 350 degrees until bubbling (about 30 minutes). Top with onion rings. Return to oven and bake until onion rings turn brown. See recipe for French Fried Onion Rings (page 96). Serve with any wild game or fowl.

Serves 8 if you give them anything else.

## Baked Stuffed Mushrooms

| | |
|---|---|
| 12 | large white mushrooms |
| 1 | large stalk celery, finely chopped |
| 1 | medium onion, finely chopped |
| 1/2 | stick butter or margarine |
| 2 | Tbs fine dry bread crumbs |
| 1/2 | tsp dried oregano |
| 1 | whole egg lightly beaten (may substitute 2 Tbs milk) |
| | salt & pepper |

Remove mushroom stems. Melt half the butter in a skillet and saute' the stems, onion and celery with the oregano. Add the bread crumbs, egg (or milk) and salt and pepper to taste. Fill mushroom caps and place on baking sheet. Dot with butter, sprinkle with additional salt and pepper and bake 15 minutes at 400 degrees. Serve with cutlets, chops, roasts, birds.

# Chive And Onion Potato Bake

1     5 1/2 oz. box hash brown potato mix with onions
4     large eggs
1     8 oz. soft cream cheese with chives & onion
1/2  Cup milk
1/3  Cup grated Parmesan cheese
1/2  tsp pepper

Rehydrate potatoes according to package directions. Drain well. With a fork or wire whisk, beat eggs, soft cream cheese and milk in a large bowl until blended. Stir in potatoes, Parmesan and pepper. Pour into lightly greased 13" x 9" baking dish or shallow 10" round casserole. Bake in preheated 350 degree oven 35-40 minutes until set and lightly browned. Let stand 5 minutes before cutting. Serve as a main dish with a tossed salad, or cut in small squares for pick-up party appetizers.

Serves 4.

# Yellow Squash Casserole

2     16 oz. cans yellow squash (1 quart frozen)
1     egg, slightly beaten
1     medium onion, chopped
1/2  bell pepper, chopped
1     jar chopped pimiento
1     10 3/4 oz. can cream of chicken soup
1     pint (8 oz.) sour cream
      salt & pepper to taste
1     stick margarine, melted
1     pkg. herb stuffing

Cook the squash, onion and bell pepper together until tender, drain. Add pimiento, soup, sour cream, salt and pepper and mash together.

Stir the herb stuffing into melted margarine. Place half of the stuffing in bottom of a greased (sprayed) 11 3/4" x 7 1/2" x 1 3/4" casserole dish. Place the squash mixture on top of the stuffing. Then cover with remainder of the stuffing. Bake at 375 degrees until hot, bubbly and browned, probably 20 minutes. Serve with roasts of venison, elk or moose.

Serves 6-8.

# Swiss Broccoli Casserole

2     10 oz. pkg. frozen broccoli spears, cooked according to pkg directions (5 minutes)
3     hard boiled eggs, sliced.
2     10 3/4 oz. cans cream of celery soup
1/2  soup can of milk
2     medium onions, sliced and French fried
1/2  Cup (about 2 oz.) shredded Swiss cheese

Mix the soup and milk right well. Arrange the cooked broccoli in an 8" x 12" lightly greased or sprayed baking dish . . . will cover the bottom. Beginning with the sliced eggs, layer the eggs, 1/2 of the French fried onions, soup/milk mixture and the Swiss cheese over the broccoli. Bake at 350 degrees for 25 minutes. Top with remaining onions and bake another 5 minutes.

Serves 8.

# Squash Casserole

3     Cups cooked squash
1     egg, slightly beaten
1/2  stick margarine, sliced
1/2  Cup mayonnaise
1     Tbs sugar
1     Cup grated cheddar cheese, divided

1 1/2 Cups cracker crumbs, divided
salt & pepper to taste
dash cayenne pepper
dash oregano

Put well-drained, hot squash in large mixing bowl. Add egg, margarine, mayonnaise, sugar, half of cheese, half of cracker crumbs, cayenne, salt and pepper and oregano. Mix well. Put into buttered 1 1/2 quart casserole and top with rest of cheese and crumbs. Bake at 350 degrees for 20 minutes.

We've used yellow straight neck and yellow crooked neck squash with the same end results . . . good. Canned squash has been substituted for fresh squash with no apparent decline in taste.

Serves 8 or 10.

# Spiced Carrots

3/4  Cup water
3     lbs. carrots, sliced 1/4 " thick
1     Cup dark seedless raisins
1/2  Cup butter or margarine

1/3  Cup finely chopped onion
2     tsp ground cinnamon
1/4  Cup packed brown sugar

Cook all ingredients over low heat (except brown sugar) in a covered 4-quart saucepan until the carrots are fork tender, stirring occasionally . . . probably 40-45 minutes. Add brown sugar; cook until sugar is dissolved. Serve with baked collared peccary, white fronted goose or fillet of Montana Widgeon.

# Po' Folks Spiced Cabbage

1   firm head of white cabbage (about 2 lbs.)
6   Tbs vegetable oil (That's .375 Cup, if you want to be technical)
6   Tbs white vinegar
4   Tbs sugar
6   whole cloves
4   large cooking apples, peeled, cored, sliced
1   tsp salt
4   Tbs (2 shot glasses) Triple Sec or Curacao

Coarse shred or thin slice the cabbage. Heat oil in large, deep skillet or Dutch oven. Add cabbage and stir to coat thoroughly with oil. Add all the remaining ingredients, stir good, and simmer (with lid on) for one (1) hour over low heat. Surprisingly good with goose, venison, duck, cottontail rabbit or spotted guinea pig.

Serves 8.

*People who don't like cabbage will require two helpings of this stuff.*

# Spicy Red Cabbage

1     medium head red cabbage, shredded
1/4   Cup cider vinegar
3/4   Cup water
1/4   tsp ground allspice
1/4   tsp ground cinnamon
1/8   tsp ground nutmeg
2     tart apples, peeled, cored, diced
1     Tbs sugar

In a saucepan, combine cabbage with next 5 items. Cover and cook over moderate heat for 20 minutes, tossing several times so cabbage will cook evenly. Add apples, toss again. Cover and cook 5 minutes more. Add sugar, toss again. Serve with any venison dish.

Serves 6.

# The Lair's Baked Beans

| | | | | |
|---|---|---|---|---|
| 2 | 16 oz cans pork and beans | 1 | ounce garlic juice |
| 1 | Cup onion rings, halved | 1 | Cup prepared barbeque sauce |
| 1 | cup thinly sliced green peppers | 2 | Tbs Karo dark corn syrup |
| 8 | bacon slices | | |

Place the beans in a Dutch oven. Fry the bacon in a skillet until crisp. Drain, crumble and add to the beans. Pour off about half of the bacon grease. Add the onion rings, sliced pepper and garlic juice to the skillet and saute until the onion is golden soft... not browned... much. Add this mess to the beans along with the molasses and barbeque sauce. Stir up real well.

Bake (uncovered) for 30 minutes at 350 degrees F... should be real bubbly and taste great.

Serves 7-8.

## Duck Camp Celery

| | | | |
|---|---|---|---|
| 4 | Cups chopped celery | 1/2 | Cup slivered almonds |
| 1 | Cup grated cheddar cheese | 2 | cans cream of celery soup |
| 1 | Cup buttered bread crumbs (browned) | | |

Cover the bottom of a greased baking dish with 2/3 of the buttered bread crumbs. Add a layer of celery, some slivered almonds and some cheese . . . then more celery, almonds and cheese until the dish is filled. Spread the cream of celery soup on top so that it covers the celery. Save a few sliced almonds and pieces of cheese to sprinkle on top of the soup. Sprinkle the remaining buttered bread crumbs on top and bake for 1 hour and 15 minutes at 325 degrees.

*Good with any wild game . . . A mainstay in the Lair of the Ancient Hunter.*

## "Oh Joy's" Garlic Grits Casserole

1 1/2 Cups quick cooking grits
     water according to directions on package
2   pkgs. Kraft Garlic Cheese
1   stick butter
5   eggs, lightly beaten
     Tabasco sauce to taste
     salt & pepper to taste
1   Cup corn flake crumbs

Cook grits according to package directions. Add other items except corn flakes and stir until well blended. Pour into casserole dish and bake for 35-45 minutes at 350 degrees.

Cover with corn flake crumbs just prior to sticking into oven.

# Cheddar Cheese And Grits Casserole

| | | | | |
|---|---|---|---|---|
| 6 | Cups water | 2 | cloves garlic, crushed |
| 1 1/2 | Cups grits | 1 | tsp paprika |
| 3 | eggs | 1/2 | tsp Tabasco |
| 2 | tsp salt | 1 | stick butter |
| 8 | oz. sharp cheddar cheese, grated | | |

Bring water to a boil in a large saucepan and stir in grits. Stir constantly until completely mixed. Cook, stirring, until thickened. Beat eggs slightly and add a small amount of grits, stirring constantly to prevent overcooking of the eggs; then add to grits. Add seasonings, cheese and butter. Mix well. Pour grits into a buttered 2-quart casserole and bake at 350 degrees for 45 minutes.

Serves 6.

# Corn Pudding

| | | | | |
|---|---|---|---|---|
| 1/4 | Cup margarine, melted | 1 | medium can whole kernel corn |
| 1/4 | Cup flour | 1 | medium can cream-style corn |
| 1/4 | Cup sugar | 2 | eggs, beaten |

Blend margarine and flour in a saucepan. Add sugar and corn; mix well. Stir in eggs. Pour into casserole. Bake 45 minutes at 350 degrees. Serve with country style doves or most anything else.

Serves 8 or thereabouts.

*This is really good and quite easy to assemble. The Good Ole Boy regulars around the Lair of the Ancient Hunter are fed a lot of it . . . goes well with all wild game dishes . . . afraid to count calories . . .*

# Sherry Poached Apples

| | | | | |
|---|---|---|---|---|
| 1/2 | Cup water | 1 | tsp vanilla |
| 2 | Cups sugar | 1/2 | Cup dry sherry |
| 2 | tsp cinnamon | | peel & juice of 1 lemon |
| 1 | stick cinnamon | 6 | large Golden Delicious apples |

Combine water, sugar, cinnamon, cinnamon stick, vanilla and sherry in heavy saucepan and cook over low heat until mixture reaches slow boil. Continue cooking and stirring occasionally.

Wash, core and peel apples. Cut in thick slices or in eighths. Poach gently in syrup until tender. Serve hot or cold with venison or other meat dishes.

Makes 6-8 servings.

# Potato Salad from the Lair of the Ancient Hunter

| | | | |
|---|---|---|---|
| 4 | Cups cubed boiled potatoes | 1/2 | tsp celery seed |
| 3 | hard boiled eggs, chopped | 1/2 | tsp salt |
| 1/2 | Cup chopped onion | 1 1/2 | Tbs prepared mustard |
| 1/2 | Cup celery slices | 1 | Cup salad dressing |
| 1/2 | Cup sweet pickle relish | | |

Mix the first five items, then mix the final four items together before mixing them with the first five. How's that for tongue twisting?

Refrigerate for 3-4 hours or even overnight before serving for best results... which will be great. Serve with most anything.

Serves 8.

# Widder Woman Sour Cream Cucumbers

| | | | |
|---|---|---|---|
| 2 | cucumbers, sliced quite thin | 1/2 | tsp salt |
| 1 | Cup sour cream | 2 | Tbs chopped chives |
| 2 | Tbs cider vinegar | 2 | Tbs chopped dill |
| 1 | Tbs sugar | 1 | tsp celery seed |

Mix all ingredients except sliced cucumbers in a large bowl. Add cucumbers, mix well and marinate in the refrigerator overnight. Serve with any wild game.

Serves 8.

# Fish-Potato Casserole

| | |
|---|---|
| 1 1/2-2 | lbs. fish fillets, anything in the freezer |
| 1 | 16 oz. pkg. frozen French-fried crinkle cut potatoes |
| 1 | 10 3/4 oz. can cream of celery soup |
| 2/3 | Cup milk |
| 1/4 | Cup mayonnaise |
| 1 | tsp curry powder |
| 1 | Tbs minced parsley (optional) |

Grease the bottom and sides of a 12" x 7 1/2" x 2" baking dish with vegetable oil. Place the thawed fillets in a single layer on the bottom of the dish. Spread the French fries on top of the fillets.

Combine soup, milk, mayonnaise and curry powder and pour the mixture over the fish and fries. Bake, uncovered, in a pre-heated 350 degree oven for 50-60 minutes until contents are really bubbling. Garnish with the parsley.

Serves 4.

# Old Folks Skellion's Thunder & Lightning

| | |
|---|---|
| 4 | carrots, chopped |
| 2 | bell peppers, chopped |
| 2 | firm tomatos, chopped |
| 4 | onions, sliced and separated into rings |
| 1 | bag radishes, sliced |
| 4 | ribs of celery, sliced |
| 2 | cucumbers, sliced about 1/8" thick |
| 6 | hot peppers, seeded, chopped |
| 3 | Cups vinegar |
| 3 | Cups water |
| 1/2 | tsp salt |
| 1/4 | tsp pepper |

Combine vinegar, water, salt, pepper and chopped hot peppers in a sauce pan. Bring to a rolling boil. Pour the hot mixture over the combined vegetables. Refrigerate overnight.

*Will eliminate constipation and free your tongue of hair.*


# Spaetzle

| | | | |
|---|---|---|---|
| 5 | Cups flour, sifted | 1 3/4 | Cups cold water |
| 3 | eggs | | |

Make a well in the flour and drop in the eggs. Mix and add the cold water. Beat till smooth. Place in refrigerator for 3-4 hours.

When ready to cook, bring a large pot of salted water to a rapid boil and drop the dough in as follows: Roll it out to 1/4" thick, then slice it into strips 1/4" wide. Cut these strips at right angles into pieces about 1" long. Drop them into the boiling water a few at a time so that the boiling does not stop. When all pieces are in, cover the pot and boil for 8-9 minutes. Remove from water. Serve with game dishes that have rich gravy to pour over the Spaetzle.

Serves 6-8.


# Bobby Joe's Fried Corn Cakes

| | | | |
|---|---|---|---|
| 2 | eggs | 1 | Cup self-rising corn meal |
| 1/4 | Cup vegetable oil | 1 | Cup self-rising flour |
| 1 1/3 | Cups milk, more maybe | 1 | Tbs sugar |

Beat eggs. Add oil and milk and beat well. Add corn meal, flour and sugar. Beat some more to get the consistency of pancake batter. Add some more milk, if necessary. Pour batter by scant 1/4 Cupfulls onto a hot oiled skillet or griddle, making a few 4" corncakes at a time. Cook until bubbly and bubbles burst; edges will look dry. With pancake turner, turn and cook until underside is golden. Place on heated platter; keep warm. Repeat, brushing skillet with more oil as needed. Great with just about any hunt breakfast.

Serves 6-8.

## Good Ole Boy Corn Cakes

| | | | | |
|---|---|---|---|---|
| 1/4 | Cup corn meal | 3/4 | Cup sweet milk |
| 1/2 | Tbs sugar | 1 | Cup flour |
| 1 | tsp salt | 2 | tsp baking powder |
| 1 | Cup boiling water | 1 | egg |

Put the corn meal, sugar, and salt in a mixing bowl and then pour the boiling water over them. Let this stand until the corn meal swells, then add the cold sweet milk. When cool, stir in the flour and baking powder and mix well. Add well beaten egg. Bake on hot griddle till cooked through and well browned.

Serves 4-6.

## Deer Camp Corn Muffins

| | | | | |
|---|---|---|---|---|
| 1 | Cup corn meal | 3/4 | Cup milk or buttermilk |
| 1 1/2 | tsp baking powder | 1 | egg |
| 1/2 | tsp salt | 3 | Tbs hot melted shortening |

Sift together dry ingredients, then add well beaten egg and milk. Add 1/2 tsp of soda if sour or buttermilk is used. To this add hot melted shortening just before baking. Put batter in hot, well greased muffin tins. Bake in oven at 400 degrees for 20 minutes.

Should make 8.

# Broccoli Cornbread

1    Pkg Jiffy Corn Muffin Mix
1    Pkg frozen chopped broccoli, cooked,drained and slightly mashed
1    Cup onion, chopped fine
1    Cup small curd cottage cheese
1    stick margarine, melted
4    eggs, beaten

Combine onion, cottage cheese and broccoli. Add eggs and mix again. Then add the muffin mix and the melted margarine.

Put in a greased casserole and bake at 350 degrees F for 25-30 minutes. or brown...and green!

Serves 6-8.

*It's better'n cake.*

# Aunt Wanda Berry's Hushpuppies

1    Cup plain flour                1    egg
1    Cup plain corn meal            2/3  Cup buttermilk
4    tsp baking powder              1/2  Cup chopped onion
1    tsp salt                       1/4  Cup bacon grease
1    tsp garlic juice

Combine all the dry ingredients and add the egg, garlic juice, buttermilk and bacon grease. Stir well.

Dip a teaspoon in cold water, scoop up a spoonful of batter and drop it into hot deep fat (370 degrees F) . Dip the spoon in cold water before each addition to the pot. Remove when 'puppies reach a golden brown... which won't be long.

Hushpuppies are a required accompaniment for catfish in the Lower Ohio Valley and points South.

# Buck's Spoon Bread

2    Cups milk                      1/4  Cup sugar
1/2  tsp salt                       4    Tbs butter
3/4  Cup cornmeal                   4    eggs, separated

In a saucepan bring the milk and salt to a boil and reduce the heat to simmer. Stir in the corn meal and continue to stir until it thickens. Add the butter and sugar. Remove from heat and beat in the egg yolks which have been slightly beaten. Allow to cool for about 4 minutes and fold in the egg whites which have been stiffly beaten.

Pour into a 1 1/2 quart buttered casserole and bake for about 40 minutes at 375 degrees F.

Serve with any wild game dish.

Serves 6.

## Hush Puppies
## From The Lair Of The Ancient Hunter

| | | | |
|---|---|---|---|
| 3/4 | Cup corn meal | 1 | tsp sugar |
| 3/4 | Cup flour | 1-2 | Tbs minced onion |
| 1 1/2 | tsp baking powder | 1 | egg |
| 1 | tsp salt | 2/3 | Cup milk |

Sift dry ingredients together. Add minced onion to dry ingredients. Beat egg and add milk, then add to the dry ingredients. Drop by teaspoons into deep fat 375 degrees and fry 3-5 minutes or until golden brown.

*About 20 hush puppy recipes were offered for inclusion in this book. We couldn't use them all . . . decided not to use any for fear of hurting a lot of feelings. However, Aunt Wanda Berry threatened us with terrible things if we didn't include her work. We have included our own recipe just to let you know women aren't the only people who know how to fry meal and onions.*

## Lucille's Sour Cream Cornbread

| | | | |
|---|---|---|---|
| 1 | Cup self rising corn meal | 1/2 | Cup sour cream |
| 2 | eggs, beaten | 1/2 | Cup cooking oil |
| 1 | tsp salt | 1 | Cup cream style corn |

Combine the ingredients, one at a time in order, beating well. Pour batter into a large, preheated greased skillet.

Bake at 450 degrees F until golden brown, about 25-30 minutes.

*Lucille Pearce, a Shelby County, Kentucky native, has spent a lifetime cooking wild stuff. You'd have trouble tagging her a "good ole girl"... but she's an accomplished cook, anyhow.*

# Meal Pie from the Dodge Firehouse

| 2 | Cups sugar | 3 | eggs |
|---|---|---|---|
| 1/2 | Cup butter | 2 | Tbs corn meal |
| 2 | Tbs milk | 2 | Tbs vinegar |
| 2 | Tbs vanilla | 1 | unbaked pie shell |

Preheat oven to 450 degrees F. Cream the sugar and butter. Add next five ingredients and blend well.

Pour the batter into an unbaked pie shell and place in oven. After 10 minutes, reduce heat to 325 degrees F and bake an additional 45 minutes.

Serves 6.

# Hoe Cake

| 1 | Cup white corn meal | | bacon drippings |
|---|---|---|---|
| 1/2 | tsp salt | | butter |
| 1/2 | Cup milk or water | | |

Mix corn meal, salt and enough boiling milk or water to make a stiff batter which will not spread much when dropped on a griddle. Each cake should be about 1/2 inch thick. Cook slowly and when browned on side next to griddle, place about 1/4 teaspoon of butter on top of each cake, turn and brown other side.

Serve with breakfast eggs and deer sausage.

Serves 4.

# Johnnycake

| 2 | Cups yellow corn meal | 4 | Cups boiling water |
|---|---|---|---|
| 2 | tsp salt | 1 | Tbs shortening |

Mix corn meal and salt. add boiling water and shortening and beat well. Spread about 1/2" thick on a greased baking pan. Bake in a 350 degrees F oven until brown..., probably 35-40 minutes. this will make two cakes about 8' in diameter.

Serve with any wild game or fish.

*Johnnycake is always as simple bread..., something most good ole boys can handle. It was originally called journey cake and was made quickly by circuit riding preachers and other travelers in early Kentucky and was baked before and open fire. If it is baked on a griddle instead of in the oven, made with white corn meal and sweetened with 2 teaspoons of sugar or molasses, it can be served on Sundays.*

# Buckwheat Cakes

4  Cups buckwheat flour
2  Cups milk, scalded
2  Cups boiling water
1  yeast cake
1/2 tsp baking soda, dissolved in 1 cup hot water
1  Tbs molasses (dark corn syrup)

Mix the milk and water in an earthen crock. Let cool to lukewarm and dissolve the yeast cake in the mixture. Sift in the flour to make a batter thin enough to pour. Let rise overnight. Come morning, add the dissolved soda, molasses and salt. Drop the batter by spoonfuls onto a heavy metal well greased griddle. Keep the heat low so the cakes will not cook too fast. When the top is full of tiny bubbles, the bottom should be brown. Turn and brown the other side.

Serve with the syrup of your choice. will make about 3 1/2 dozen cakes.

# Firehouse Biscuits

8 Cups flour     1 Cup Crisco
4 Cups buttermilk   2 Tbs sugar
4 Tbs baking powder 1 Tbs salt
1 tsp soda

Sift flour, add other dry ingredients, mix well and cut in Crisco. Add buttermilk slowly and knead well. Roll the dough out on a flour covered board. Cut with a flour covered biscuit cutter. Bake at 400 degrees F in a greased pan until brown.

Makes about 30.

*This recipe is the result of nearly a half century of biscuit making by one Leon Dodge, Fat Jolly good ole boy Fire Chief of Paducah, Kentucky. His proudest moment came when he was selected as the model for the Pillsbury Doughboy. His ladder climbing career was ended by decree of the City Council. Ladders structurally strong enough to handle him were costing more than the Fire House Pension Fund.*

# Broccoli Soup from the House of John

| | | | | |
|---|---|---|---|---|
| 11/2 | lb broccoli, chopped | 1 | pinch of basil, sage and thyme |
| 1 | qt chicken stock or broth | 1 | dash of Tabasco |
| 1/4 | lb margarine | 2 | Cups milk |
| 1/2 | medium onion, chopped | 1/2 | Cup heavy cream |
| 1 | bay leaf | 1 | Cup buttermilk |
| 3/4 | tsp salt | 7 | Tbs flour |
| 3/4 | tsp white pepper | 3 | Tbs sour cream |
| 1/4 | tsp onion salt | 1/4 | lb butter, melted |
| 1/4 | tsp garlic salt | | |

In a large pot, bring stock to a boil and add the chopped broccoli. Bring back to a boil, cover. Lower heat to low and simmer until broccoli is almost done..., about 10 minutes.

Saute onions in 2 tablespoons of the margarine until translucent and add to the stock along with the seasonings. Simmer until vegetables are done... about 10 minutes.

In the meantime, combine the milk, cream and buttermilk and warm in a saucepan.

In another saucepan, over low heat, melt the remaining 6 tablespoons of margarine, add flour and whisk constantly for a couple of minutes. Add the warmed liquids and stir until the mixture is thickened. Gradually add thickened liquids to stock and stir. Soup should be very hot but not boiling. Remove bay leaf. Turn off heat, stir in sour cream and melted butter. Serve.

Serves 6-8.


# Cousin Sallee's Famous Cheese Ball

| | | | | |
|---|---|---|---|---|
| 3 | 8 oz pkg cream cheese | 1 | sm jar dried beef ( chopped fine) |
| 4 | green onions | 1 | Cup pecans, chopped |

Remove 1" from the bulb end of the onions and discard it. Chop the rest (including tops) of the onions finely and mix with the cream cheese and chopped dried beef. Form into a ball and roll it in the chopped pecans. Refrigerate for 4 hours. Serve with cocktail crackers of your choice.

*Cousin Sallee Campbell is a gourmet though frustrated cook. Frustration is result of years of unsuccessful effort to convert good ole boy husband into something her mother would favor.*

# Spicy Cocktail Deerballs

| | | | | |
|---|---|---|---|---|
| 2 | lb ground venison | 1/3 | Cup tomato catsup |
| 1 | Cup packaged corn flake crumbs | 2 1/2 | Tbs instant minced onions |
| 1/3 | dried parsley flakes | 1 | lb can jellied cranberry sauce |
| 2 | eggs | 2 | Tbs  packed dark brown sugar |
| 2 | Tbs soy sauce | 1 | Tbs lemon juice |
| 1/4 | tsp black pepper | 1 | 12 oz bottle chile sauce |
| 1/2 | tsp garlic salt | | |

Preheat oven to 350 degrees F.

in a large mixing bowl combine first 10 ingredients.  Mix well.  Form the ground venison in small balls and place them on a cookie sheet or bread pan at least 1" deep.

Combine the remaining ingredients in a medium size saucepan over medium heat.   Stir often until mixture is smooth and cranberry sauce is melted.  Pour over deerballs and bake uncovered for 30 minutes.   Keep warm while serving with toothpicks.

Will make about 60.


# Sweet Vegetable Relish

| | | | | |
|---|---|---|---|---|
| 12 | medium onions | 4 | Cups sugar |
| 1 | medium head cabbage | 2 | Tbs mustard seed |
| 10 | green tomatos | 1 | Tbs celery seed |
| 12 | green peppers | 1 1/2 | tsp turmeric |
| 6 | sweet red peppers | 4 | generous Cups cider vinegar |
| 1/2 | Cup salt | 2 | Cups water |

Grind vegetables using a coarse blade. (There should be about 5 cups each of ground onions, cabbage and tomatos.) Sprinkle with salt. Let stand overnight. Rinse and drain. Combine remaining ingredients and pour over vegetables. Bring to a boil; reduce heat and simmer 3 minutes. Divide among 8 sterilized pint jars, leaving 1/2-inch head space. There should be enough liquid to cover; add extra vinegar if necessary. Seal.

Serve with any venison dish . . . and dried beans, et al.

# Four Vegetable Relish

2 1/2  pounds green peppers (about 12 medium)
1      small head cabbage (1 pound)
1      pound onions (3-4 large)
1      pound carrots (7 medium)
2 3/4  Cups Heinz Distilled White Vinegar
3/4    Cup water
1 1/2  Cups granulated sugar
3      Tbs salt
1      Tbs mustard seed
1      Tbs celery seed

Wash, trim and quarter vegetables. Put vegetables through food grinder using coarse blade; drain, discarding liquid. Combine vinegar and remaining ingredients in large saucepot; heat to boiling. Add vegetables; simmer 5 minutes, stirring occasionally. Continue simmering while quickly packing one clean, hot jar at a time. Fill to within 1/2 inch of top making sure vinegar solution covers vegetables. Cap each jar at once. Process 5 minutes in boiling-water bath. Makes 5-6 pints.

# Dill Pickles

4      pounds 4-inch pickling cucumbers
1/4    Cup salt
2 3/4  Cups Heinz Distilled White Vinegar
3      Cup water
12-14  sprigs fresh dill weed
28     peppercorns

Wash cucumbers; cut in half lengthwise. Combine salt, vinegar and water; heat to boiling. Pack cucumbers into clean jars. Add 2 sprigs dill weed and 4 peppercorns to each jar. Pour vinegar solution over cucumbers to within 1/2 inch of top. Immediately adjust covers as jar manufacturer directs. Process 10 minutes in boiling-water bath. Makes 6-7 pints.

# Zucchini Pickles

1      quart Heinz Distilled White Vinegar
2      Cups granulated sugar
1/4    Cup salt
2      tsp celery seed
2      tsp ground turmeric
1      tsp dry mustard
5      pounds (5-6 inch) zucchini, unpeeled, cut into 1/4-inch slices
1      quart thinly sliced onions (4-5 medium)

Combine first 6 ingredients in saucepan; bring to boil. Pour over zucchini and onions; let stand 1 hour, stirring occasionally. In saucepot, bring mixture to a boil, then simmer 3 minutes. Continue simmering while quickly packing one clean, hot jar at a time. Fill to within 1/2 inch of top making sure vinegar solution covers vegetables. Cap each jar at once. Process 5 minutes in boiling-water bath.

Makes 6-7 pints.

## Cranberry Chutney

| | | | |
|---|---|---|---|
| 1 | 16 oz. package cranberries | 1 | Cup English walnuts |
| 2 | Cups sugar | 1 | Cup chopped celery |
| 1 | Cup water | 1 | Cup seedless raisins |
| 1 | Cup orange juice | 1 | medium apple, cored, chopped |
| 1 | Tbs grated orange peel | 1 | tsp ground ginger |

Heat cranberries, sugar and water to boiling, stirring often. Reduce heat to low and simmer 15 minutes. Remove from heat, stir in other ingredients. Cover and refrigerate.

Serves 10-12. Serve with any wild game.

## Peach Chutney

3   pounds peaches, slightly underripe
1   quart water +1 Tbs vinegar
1   Cup firmly packed light brown sugar
3/4   Cup seedless raisins
3/4   Cup honey
3/4   Cup Heinz Distilled White Vinegar
1/4   tsp mace
6   whole cloves
1   (3-inch) cinnamon stick, broken up

Pour boiling water over peaches; let stand until skins can be easily removed. Dip in cold water; peel. Remove pits and red fibers; cut into chunks. Place immediately in vinegar-water to prevent browning. In saucepan combine brown sugar and next 4 ingredients. Add cloves and cinnamon tied in cheesecloth bag. Drain peaches; add to syrup. Simmer 1 hour, stirring occasionally. Remove spice bag. Continue simmering while quickly packing one clean hot jar at a time. Fill to within 1/2 inch of top making sure syrup covers fruit. Seal each jar at once. Process 5 minutes in boiling-water bath.

Makes 4-5 half pints. Serve as part of any wild game menu.

# Cousin Ann's Slaw

1    head of green cabbage, shredded
1/2  head of purple cabbage, shredded
2    medium onions, chopped
1    green pepper, shopped
1    Cup vinegar
11/2 Cups sugar
1    tsp celery seed
3/4  Cup cooking oil
1    Tbs salt
1    tsp dry mustard

Mix cabbage, onion and green pepper in storage container. Mix vinegar, sugar, celery seed, salt, and mustard in sauce pan and heat to a boil. Add oil and mix well. Pour over cabbage mixture and mix well. Cover tightly and refrigerate overnight. Serve with any red meat.

Serves 6-8.

# Special Tips

**"Bet No. 6 to win in the 7th race at Bluegrass Downs."**

# Special Tips

☞ The meat of antlered animals is generally referred to as venison, especially deer meat. The fat of these animals is strongly flavored and should be trimmed from the meat before freezing or cooking. They should never be cooked in their own fat. Barding, the covering of roasts with fat, bacon or salt pork, is recommended to prevent dryness and add juiciness. Larding, or sticking slivers of fat meat into the meat with a special needle also gets the job done. However, the process is probably too complicated for most good ole boys. Basting with butter , margarine or bacon drippings is best for chops, cutlets and steaks.

If you're going to broil them on a charcoal grill, douse them with a little grocery store meat tenderizer an hour ahead of grilling. Cook quickly. Serve on a hot platter. Less tender cuts of venison can be used in various recipes calling for ground meat.

☞ Bears, wild boar and javelina should be treated like pork ... cooked to an internal temperature of 150 degrees F or more for they are known to carry trichinosis on occasion. This is bad. The javelina has a musk sac in the rear-center of its back which must be removed at the earliest possible time during field dressing. After skinning and fat trimming, soak the carcass in a vinegar-water solution for a couple of hours before cooking or freezing.

☞ It takes a brave man to open a bear's stomach and most hunters try to avoid this during field dressing. However, it's a good idea to do so if you think there's a chance your bear may have been eating long dead or decaying fish. You can't eliminate the fishy taste. Better hope you have a trophy hide.

☞ The word "marinate" means "to pickle" or preserve, soften and flavor . . . and marinating does just that. Ideally, there should be enough marinade to cover. However half-way up is alright provided the meat or birds is turned frequently. The marinade should also be stirred at each turning and only glass, ceramic or porcelain containers should be used. The acid in most marinades will eat on metals, alas.

☞ Roast and broiled meat of antlered animals may be cooked rare (140 degrees F), medium (160 degrees F), or well done (170 degrees F) according to taste. Since cooking times vary from oven to oven (or oven thermometers do), it is a good idea to use a meat thermometer which is inserted into thickest part of the meat. It should never rest against the bone.

☞ Never pour black coffee into an intoxicated fisherman. You'll probably wind up with a wide awake drunk on your hands.

☞ A lot of game is ruined because it is kept in the freezer too long. Venison (deer, moose, elk, antelope, caribou) has enjoyed all the freezer time it needs in 10 months. Rabbit, squirrel, boar, muskrat, peccary, raccoon and groundhog will deteriorate badly after 6 months in the freezer. Ducks and geese should be used within 4 months of freezing. Quail, woodcock, grouse and pheasant can take about 6 months of freezer time unless you freeze them in water which will double acceptable freezer time.

☞ Meat frozen and maintained at 0 degrees F or colder will lose none of its good flavor.

☞ Meat to be frozen should be cut into pieces ready for cooking and wrapped separately.

☞ If two or more pieces (like chops or steaks are to be placed in one package, they should be separated by two layers of plastic film or other moisture proof material. It makes it easy to separate them. Each package should be labeled immediately upon wrapping . . . lest we forget.

☞ Frozen meats can be cooked immediately upon removal from the freezer. However, it does better when thawed and the slower the thawing the better. Meat will thaw at the rate of 2 hours per pound at room temperature. In the refrigerator, about 5 hours per pound is required.

☞ There is probably no better way to loaf, without attracting criticism and unfavorable attention, than to go fishing.

☞ When freezing fish for future use, a constant temperature of -5 degrees F to -10 degrees F assures best results. At these temperatures lean fish may be stored for 9-12 months; medium fat fish for 5-9 months; and fatty fish for 3-4 months. Freezer life can be extended by 9-12 months by block freezing. Milk or ice cream cartons, anything that will contain water will suffice. Be sure the fish is covered.

☞ Roasts of all kinds as well as large birds are more easily carved, if they are allowed to stand for 15-20 minutes before applying the knife.

☞ Birds and portions of animals that have been "shot up" badly should be soaked in salt water for several hours to overnight prior to freezing or cooking. Won't hurt to put them in the refrigerator during the soaking.

☞ You can assure yourself a better tasting opossum, if you take it alive and feed it a diet of vegetables for 2-3 days before butchering. 'Possums not fed the controlled diet should be soaked in salt water overnight before being cooked.

☞ Any recipe for cooking a wild goose that contains oranges, orange juice, orange marmalade or orange anything will probably turn out great.

☞ When deepfrying fish, the ideal temperature of the fat is 370-380 degrees F. If you do not have a cooking thermometer, bring the fat to "smoking" temperature, then lower heat until the smoking stops. At this temperature whole small fish or pieces up to 1 1/2" thick will be completely cooked and browned in about 5 minutes. Fish should be added a few at a time to keep the fat temperature even. Handle the fish with tongs. Drain the fish on cloth or paper towels for a few minutes before serving.

# The Cook

Uncle Russ Chittenden was a member of the first graduating class of the Kentucky College of Hunting and Fishing. Lesser known classmates included D. Boone, S. Kenton, J.J. Audubon, G.R. Clark . . . He has spent a lifetime hunting, fishing, birdwatching, camping and just lost in the woods.

Advancing age has slowed him a little. He still collects about as many quail, doves, ducks and geese as he ever did . . . has just supplemented failing eyesight with a finely developed ability to claim dead birds. His wing shooting seems to be best when he's seated between two good shots.

His offbeat writings have appeared in a large number of outdoor publications, countless southern and midwestern newspapers and on numerous public restroom walls. A long time male chauvinist, he has mellowed in recent years to the extent he now allows his woman, "Allison", to run things . . . like the vacuum cleaner, washing machine, and lawnmower . . ., even lets her go to Women's Lib meetings as long as she's home in time to cook supper and get the milking done.

A sometimes camp cook from boyhood, Unc started cooking seriously when his woman became serious about the Women's Lib stuff and joined in their national "Starve A Rat" Program . . ., and with a pile of unskinned varmints on hand, too.

Cooking smells coming out of his "Lair of the Ancient Hunter" regularly set off smoke alarms in four states and causes air pollution indexes to rise sharply. The Lair is the home of the Thirty First Street Philosophical and Cut Bait Society. Members gather here regularly to make pleasant conversation about girls, politics, bird dogs, religion, Ducks Unlimited, fishing, girls, boats, motors, whiskey, beer, girls, the NRA, etc. Uncle Russ has served faithfully as both Grand Philosopher and Master Baiter.

A semi-retired civil engineer/cartographer type, Unc is quite well read in a number of other fields. It is said he knows enough about biology, zoology, botany, geology and all that stuff to discuss same with most college professors . . . and enough about engineering to be dangerous. As someone said about the late W.C. Fields, "any man who hates dogs and children can't be all bad."

# Index